JOSEPH IN

To Cristina Kirkwood
from Ruth Philip
October 13th 2018

In Memory of My Husband Maxwell Philip
For Jane and Martin, Gavin, Katie and Donald

JOSEPH IN EGYPT

A PLAY IN A PROLOGUE AND FOUR ACTS

BY

RUTH PHILIP

First printed in 2018 by
Bell & Bain Limited
303 Burnfield Road, Thornliebank
Glasgow G46 7UQ

ISBN 978-1-5272-2092-8

Typeset by Palimpsest Book Production Limited,
Falkirk, Stirlingshire

INTRODUCTION

Line drawings of Egyptian gods occupied several pages of my mother's Bible and so were familiar to me as a child. Many years later I began to read about Ancient Egypt with keen interest and to consider the first world drama known to me with a happy ending – Joseph's adventures in Genesis. As I wrote individual poems 'spoken' by each of the members of the cast at different moments in their journey, one by one they came alive for me and this led me to complete their story. 'Joseph in Egypt' is the result.

Most of the poems which form the framework are written in blank verse, sometimes strict, sometimes not, using modern words in an ordinary word order, avoiding the temptation of older-style phrasing (Elizabethan/Jacobean) such as: 'Let not your heart be troubled, neither be afraid', an iambic *hex*ameter from John 14.

The iambic foot in poetry, with its stress on the second syllable, carries the mind forward with a sense of urgency, of excited anticipation, which is why it has always been so popular among writers in English. It is marvellous for heightening drama, for lending a sense of wonder and glory, for soaring.

I wrote poems in free style as well, hoping always that a line would achieve 'a perfect imperfection of its own', to quote Anne Ridler's delightful thought.

To share my love of Ancient Egypt, I included a myriad details of life in the ancient world – making of 'Joseph' a sort of mini-encyclopaedia. This is most apparent in Act I, where Potiphar's household typifies the everyday behaviour and preoccupations of his world. The only liberty taken here was to put a cone of wax (looking like a large Red Indian feather) on the head of the Egyptian women at an aristocratic party. These aren't shown until New Kingdom paintings, which would appear to be of later date than Joseph.

The sketch of Joseph's investiture as vizier in Act II and the short scenes which give a hint of one or two of his responsibilities are wholly authentic, but while Pharaoh must make a monumental entry, I envisage the scenes in Act II, other than the love scenes, as taken mainly at a brisk pace. A vigorous delivery here would provide a bridge to the second part of Joseph's story, which begins in Act III, for, like the novel 'Great Expectations', Joseph's drama is made up of two distinct parts.

The typical Ancient Egyptian crime of shifting boundary stones to claim more land is universal. In the mid-eighteen hundreds in rural France Rimbaud's mother made a habit of it. Even if someone wishes to cut out the criminal proceedings in Act II for a reading or performance of the play, Joseph's speech in the law court: 'Do not swear by Pharaoh' can never be omitted because it explains to everyone what a tremendous oath Joseph is using when he swears 'By the life of Pharaoh', the authentic Ancient Egyptian oath quoted in Genesis, as he rails at his brothers.

I have placed Joseph the man in the second Intermediate period, where the Hyksos, Semitic rulers, whose origin is still disputed, were surely the pharaohs most likely to promote a fellow-Semite to the highest rank in the kingdom. They may have invaded from either Phoenicia or southern Arabia and appear to have made a bad start before taking on the values of Egyptian civilisation. I have chosen the name of a real pharaoh within this period, one about whom, as yet, nothing appears to be known.

If this placing of Joseph is correct, it may explain why there is no trace of Joseph, so far, in Egyptian archaeology. The Ancient Egyptian word for ‘Egyptian’ was also the word for ‘person’. The Egyptians tended to be xenophobic, resenting even benefits from a foreign source. In the case of the Hyksos, originally intruders, they obliterated all records as soon as they could, following their tradition of chiselling unwanted names out of stone tablets and monuments.

Some of my writing in ‘Joseph’ I think of as ‘poetry of fact’. The little poem about the grey heron or bennu bird in the love scene which is the coloured centrefold of ‘Joseph in Egypt’ is inspired by my discovery that the apparent disappearance and reappearance of the bird in the early morning sun in Ancient Egypt is the sole origin and source of the legend of the phoenix.

‘Joseph’ is a tale without limits. How amazing it is to see that Genesis, the first book of the Bible, shows in this story the moment where three world religions of similar moral ideals all meet for the first time. Like a paternal God, Joseph’s father Jacob has mercy on his ten sons. This fable is the ancient harbinger of the Christian parable of the prodigal son. ‘The Kingdom of Heaven is like this.’ I hope in my retelling of ‘Joseph’ I have shown the harmony between all three revelations, all three ideals of human conduct, as part of the background to the family saga.

I preferred to temper this serious drama with comedy, especially in the last three acts. Essentially the Prologue is a tragedy, while Act I, centred on Potiphar’s wife’s pursuit of Joseph, is nothing but comedy. She must have been a foolish woman, for success could have led to an excruciating death penalty in this life and being eaten by a crocodile twice in the next.

Her persecution of Joseph can stand alone as a one act play, if so wished, a comedy of Ancient Egyptian manners.

It was this woman’s false accusation that sent Joseph into an indefinite prison sentence and from this, as has happened in a more recent African life story, he emerged as a wise statesman and ruler intent upon mercy and reconciliation. Somehow this later history adds to Joseph’s credibility, already made tremendously strong by his swearing ‘By the life of Pharaoh’ in the dialogue given in Genesis.

Retelling this magnificent saga became a need for me as I explored Ancient Egypt and Ancient Canaan in books. I tried to complete the emotions, the words and thoughts that are partly indicated in Genesis. It was an enthralling quest in which I delighted.

Joseph's story is the world's first real romance known to me. The epic drama culminates in overwhelming remorse and godlike forgiveness. Judah's horror at his own actions cannot leave a dry eye in the house and all unite in love.

I first regarded 'Joseph in Egypt' as complete more than twenty years ago, but have shortened it since. I am publishing it now for my daughter and her husband and for my grandchildren as a memento. Chiefly I intend it as a memorial to my dear husband Max who, after reading it, made only one comment: 'It is a noble work and deserves success'.

Ruth Philip
Glasgow, U.K.
March 2018

ACKNOWLEDGEMENTS

When I finished 'Joseph in Egypt' over twenty years ago I at once asked a friend who is a Wordsworth expert to vet it. She thought highly of the poetry but advised me to ask someone else to assess it as drama and queried whether it might offend the Jewish community. So I must thank Katy Myers for her first encouraging reaction to my writing, Margaret Tomlinson for finding it 'valid' as drama and Lady Clarice Goldberg for reassuring me that my portrayal of the patriarchs was unlikely to offend.

Re-reading 'Joseph' recently and looking at the play from a producer's point of view, Margaret thought I should stress that, although this is a man's story, there are very strong, even 'feisty' women in it, most rewarding parts for women that you would not expect. I am also glad she remarked that, in her view, all the obvious difficulties posed by Joseph's large and varied cast can be overcome and there is nothing to make production impossible.

Praise for the 'speakability' of 'Joseph in Egypt' came from Hugh Hodgart and my tutor Olive Sayce found the interplay of characters and the depiction of everyday life admirable. Recently I was grateful for kind words, 'insightful', 'genial', from Denise Steel, who even noticed the theology of the play. I am indebted to Elizabeth McKenzie for the photograph on the back cover and to Paddy Hanrahan for the design on the front cover that will almost compel people to open the book and read it. Lastly I wish to express my appreciation to Grace Gunnell for her continuing interest in my script and her insistence that I should do something with it. My grateful thanks go to all who have given me generous encouragement, including those who let me know they had enjoyed reading 'Joseph' aloud to each other.

So now I am sending 'Joseph' out into the world. As a very private person I may wish I hadn't, but if Ben Jonson could take all the flak he received for publishing his Complete Plays in 1616, I can probably stand up to whatever comes my way.

Ruth Philip

JOSEPH IN EGYPT

LIST OF CHARACTERS

IN CANAAN

JACOB	The Hebrew Patriarch	His five middle sons:
REUBEN)		Dan and Naphtali
SIMEON)		Gad and Asher
LEVI)	His four eldest sons	Issachar
JUDAH)		
LEAH	His wife	
DINAH	His daughter	
ZEBULUN	His tenth son	
BENJAMIN	His twelfth, youngest son	

IN EGYPT

JOSEPH	Jacob's eleventh son	Pharaoh's baker
POTIPHAR	Captain of the palace guard	Pharaoh's butler
ANHAI	Potiphar's wife	A Syrian seer
SENEB	A soldier	A Libyan
KIYA	Seneb's wife	A palace official
SIMONIDES	A Greek slave	A granary overseer
KHYAN	The young Pharaoh	An interpreter

NEKHEBU	Pharaoh's councillor	A constable, a judge
ASENATH	Joseph's bride	and guests, guards,
TUYA	Asenath's companion	fan-bearers, servants,
INTEF	Joseph's steward	criminals, officials

PROLOGUE IN CANAAN

THE LIE

SCENE I

A rocky hillock close to grazing land at Dothan, from which occasional bleating may be heard. Nine of Joseph's ten elder brothers are talking in groups, Judah, their leader, with Simeon and Levi; Dan with Naphtali, Gad and Asher; Issachar with Zebulun. Enter Reuben, Jacob's first born son.

JUDAH (*scathingly*) And here comes Reuben, hotfoot from the brothel.
The hot-eyed lecher has returned to us,
Remembering our father's flocks and herds
And all his brothers. Welcome, Reuben.
Why, Reuben, you're distraught.

REUBEN (*urgently*) The cistern's empty.
Just tell me, Judah. You've hauled Joseph up
And sent him home to Jacob. Am I right?
The well is smooth below the grooves cut by
Long centuries of straining shepherds' ropes –
Our brother couldn't have managed without help.
And at the dry well's foot I only saw
The drifts of leaves. Judah, what did you do

With that half-naked, shivering, sobbing boy?
You must have tired of your bullying
And sent him home.

JUDAH (*savagely*) We hauled him up
But he will never see our camp again.
Like a snake bite we have cut him out;
To stop the poison spreading we have hacked
Him from our body! Reuben, we have sold him!

REUBEN (*explosively*) *You've* sold *Jo*seph?

JUDAH (*brightly*) Midianites from Gilead
Came this way, er – traders in gum tragacanth
And myrrh – and slaves. They gave a good price for
A supple, snivelling seventeen-year-old,
Quite dirty; chained his wrists – and roped him to
A Cappadocian donkey.

REUBEN Mad heart! Granite heart!
Wretched use you make of the authority
You won from me! Shame on you, Judah!

JUDAH He was a curse on all his brothers' lives.

REUBEN Not on mine.
Not on his young brother Benjamin's.
Nor on any of your lives. He's innocent
Of all wrong-doing. You chose resentment where
You should have chosen love.

SIMEON (*angrily*) Resentment's natural. He told tales of Gad
And Asher, Naphtali and Dan, saying they were . . .

REUBEN Neglectful herdsmen, Simeon, which they were
And I have been these two whole days. How unwise
Our Jacob was to send truth-telling Joseph on
That errand. So – this time, when Jacob sent
Him out to bring back news of us, you threw
Him in a well and sold him! – Senseless! –
Come, Judah. We must travel in his wake
And buy him back.

SIMEON Ah! Just try that, brother Reuben!

REUBEN (*intensely*) Simeon, as
You hope for mercy, let me save the boy!

SIMEON I'll never need it! Mercy? No man stands
His ground when I appear with Levi. We
Inspire fear wherever we are known.

REUBEN (*reproachfully*) Judah, *you* should have prevented this!

JUDAH (*dryly*) Remember, Simeon slays like a berserker.
You know that Levi is his echo. We hear
About berserkers through the amber trade. Joseph's
Halfway to the Negev with the caravan –
Alive – because I overruled the rest. (*sardonically*)
Just think! The merchants marvelled at our lack
Of empty stomachs. – *Hunger's* generally
Why relatives are sold. Be satisfied
That I prevented Joseph's death! (*angrily*) In my
View, his enslavement is the punishment
Of all his pride!

REUBEN (*vigorously*) Not pride! The confidence
Of one beloved of fortune and his father,

Not guessing how his privilege offends
His brothers. *Joy* of young, spoilt, next-to-last
Born son, who thinks his older brothers all
Agree a policy of cosseting
For love of him. How can I make you see!
There's no way we can tell our father he's unjust.
Such an insult is considered worthy
Of death. Traditions of unquestioning
Obedience seal our lips. Ten times more than us,
He loves his Rachel's first-born – ten times more.
What can we do? Accept – and grumble now and then
Well out of earshot of the Patriarch.
What happens? We are all hot-blooded men
And violent-tempered; therefore, we improve
On this and seethe and bubble round our boiling point
For days and weeks – till suddenly we see
Our hurts, self-dealt, are trivial.

JUDAH (*angrily*) I don't
Accept that! Trivial! Eleventh born
And Jacob says each day: 'This is my greatest son,
A visionary whose prophetic dreams
Reveal a special destiny. God tells
Our Joseph of a future glory in this life.'
He next reminds us we'll be wheatsheaves in
A stubble field, bowing low to Joseph as
A more important wheatsheaf. Then he recounts
His Joseph's second dream, where all the ten of us
Here now at Dothan, and with Benjamin –
Who's now in Hebron – out of our way, thank heaven,
And ignorant of what we've done – where all
Eleven of us, I say, are stars in heaven;
This dream casts Mother Leah as the moon

And Father Jacob as the Sun. In *this*
Dream, Joseph is celestially more
Important than the sun and moon – Why not ? –
For, once again, we all prostrate ourselves
In veneration of the second-youngest boy,
Our brother, the phenomenon, far greater than
The lamps of day or night! Every day, or so
It seems, our father marvels loud and long,
And in the selfsame words. More recently,
He's maddened us by buying an exquisitely
Expensive garment, long-sleeved, brightly striped,
In which the second-youngest goes parading up
And down amid his drab and well-worn brothers.
Not to be born! We can't protest, but we can do!

SIMEON (*gloatingly*) And now he's ruined.

REUBEN Hard hearts! Rogues! I loved
The boy, while you – you were always thinking of
Your injured pride, fostering your jealousy
And spite. You – you fools! Blind idiots!
Have you forgotten you recover from
Your rages? Will no other man among
You here remember that his sane self loves
The boy? Still this savaging of Joseph's life
Can be undone. Think of him stumbling through
The Negev, trudging onward in his chains,
His tears! The lad deserves your utmost pity. Save
Him, rescue him! He will embrace you, weeping on
Your shoulders. He'll forgive – and promise us
His silence. He'll not tell our father – and
Will understand us now, and do his best
To see we're less provoked to envy.

SIMEON (*angrily*) He'd torment
Us more, not less.

REUBEN Don't judge by yourself.
He's better.

JUDAH I say – the matter's splendid as
It stands, with Joseph *excised* from our lives.
You're overruled, outvoted nine to one.

REUBEN (*furiously*) Then I despair of you! Look at you!
An army of grown bearded men exulting now
Because you have destroyed the best of us,
The best of your own blood! Look at us!
Can you wonder Jacob idolised the boy?
You've proved him right! What's left now?
Only *shoddy*!
The noblest, most courageous son has gone!

SIMEON Courageous? Joseph wept like Dinah in the night
We hacked to death her violator!

REUBEN (*in exasperation*) Faced with your insanity, of course
He wept, in terror and bewilderment.
What monsters! He's well rid of us, but what
Is to become of Jacob?

JUDAH (*violently*) Don't you dare
Tell Jacob! If you do – you accuse yourself
And us. You're implicated! If you meant
To help him, why were you so long away?

REUBEN You all know why! (*wearily*) Why did Almighty God
Create a man like me? I am a stream

Of fiery lava that cools to a dead landscape of
Remorse. Once I defiled my father's bed.
In my agony of lust I seized the mother of
My brothers Dan and Naphtali; red-hot,
I violated Bilhah and became,
In all men's eyes, an object of revulsion,
Forfeiting to Judah my authority,
My rights as first-born. Judah's fourth in line,
And reigns. And now through lust I have lost all
The hours, where, rescuing Joseph secretly,
I could have brought him quietly to Jacob.
Desire welled so strong in me that I
Forgot my brother's misery. (*vigorously*) This is
The worst of all my reasons for self-hate!
(*resignedly*) What story will you tell our father?

SIMEON We've kept the robe that angered us, *his* robe.
We'll slash it, spatter it with blood, carry it
To Jacob's tents and ask our father if he thinks,
As we do, that some beast has killed the boy.

REUBEN (*wildly*) Judah, you'll let Simeon do this
To Jacob? You will leave the man no hope?
(*suddenly resigned*) True. What other story could you tell?
Poor Joseph, born into a nest of villains! – God
In his mercy bless the boy and comfort him.
As for us, we shall not be forgiven, nor,
I prophesy, shall we forgive ourselves. (*quietly*)
Thank heaven for the poor boy's sleep, his hours
Of peace, his blessed hours of forgetting.

SCENE II

Jacob's Camp at Hebron. There are sounds of bustle offstage – clanking of cooking pots, crackling flames, women's and children's voices. Leah and Dinah are sitting on the ground. They hold spindles on which they have been spinning thread from sheep's wool.

LEAH (*anxiously*) Our Joseph should have come with news of all
My sons. I am on edge. The air seems full
Of warning, as if raiders were approaching.

DINAH (*soberly*) But everything appears as usual, mother.

LEAH Beloved Dinah, what is left for you to fear?

DINAH Not much. I am broken into fragments, like
A desert of small stones. What a tale!

LEAH Your brothers' tragic act –

DINAH Schechem's tragic
Act came first, the action of a beast.
I thought him harmless as he followed me,
A youthful prince, who hoped to speak to me.
Then – running feet, his red, distorted face
Brought utter terror – I was gripped, thrown down,
My body brutalised. From far away
I looked out at a crying creature, made
Of pain and shame, who stumbled home and told
Her father, who in fury told her brothers.

LEAH Then came Hamor, father of Prince Shechem,
And suggested marriage. His son, he said,
Abhorred his crime. He would 'be kind to Dinah
All his life. All Schechem City will atone,'
Said Hamor. 'Circumcision of our men
We offer as a token. Forgive us.
We will intermarry with your tribe.
We'll make amends.'

DINAH (*controlled*) And Jacob grudgingly
Forgave them, so he said, although his look was grim.
So Hamor went away with confidence.
I went to live in Shechem Palace, home
Of Hamor and his son, and Schechem wept
And knelt before me, promising to make
Me joyful. I began to guess that peace
Might flower from his horrible assault
And that his penitence might teach me love.
I forgot my brothers' gloomy passions,
The clouds of anger in my father's tents.
I'd no foreboding, mother, at this time –
And not before my rape. It was that alone
My brothers thought of, disregarding all
Heartfelt repentance and remorse.

LEAH They feigned forgiveness while they planned revenge.

DINAH I'd no foreboding, Leah, on that night
When Simeon and Levi slaughtered sleeping men.
As Levi tore my man from where he lay
Beside me, I awoke in terror, heard
A frenzied voice roar: 'Blood must flow! Kill, kill!'
I started up and in the wavering torchlight
Saw muscles taut in Levi's arm that crushed

Poor Shechem's throat, and Simeon's savage eyes,
His knife already stained with Schechem's blood,
His bloodstained knife, already used to wound him.
I begged for Shechem's life . . .

LEAH (*murmuring*) In vain, in vain.

DINAH (*violently*) When was Simeon ever merciful
To man or beast? (*wearily*) He made his kill. Long
hours
I sat in darkness, *crad*-l-*ing* dead Shechem on
My lap, all drenched in my love's blood, and in
My ears rang shrieks from other murders of
Men ill from circumcision, dying groans;
Till only widows wailed their grief to heaven.
A swarm of other brothers came to loot.
At dawn, they dragged me from my husband's corpse
And brought me to the unending, barren shame
Of my existence here.

LEAH (*under her breath*) Poor Dinah.

DINAH I stay at home, unmarriageable, unrespected,
The servant of the brothers who have slain
My prince and made my tribe's name execrated
In the whole of Canaan. It is a bitter fate.

LEAH Worse than mine, which I found difficult
Enough, when I was young. Jacob was cheated.
I was the instrument. It was not my fault,
Though I was not unwilling, for I loved him.

DINAH Your father Laban was remarkable
For avaricious cunning.

LEAH (*gives a bitter laugh*) Yes, he loved
To overreach his fellow men. Rebecca,
Jacob's mother, was Laban's *sister*,
But Laban, tempted, drove the shrewdest of
Hard bargains to exploit the young man's love,
His adoration of . . .

DINAH Your sister Rachel.
For seven years Jacob worked without reward,
To earn the right to marry your young sister.

LEAH It was a joy to him to do it! (*with nostalgia*)
And after seven years there came the wedding day
Of Jacob and his Rachel. Now, in all
The ceremonies and the feasting
Rachel was the bride, but in the night,
While Rachel wept and howled with fury,
Laban made me go to Jacob's bed,
To Jacob's *marriage* bed in Rachel's place.

DINAH I've heard your sister taunt you, seen her toss
Her head and say: 'He did not need the help
Of darkness to choose me!'

LEAH Ah! Still that's near
The bone! My ardent husband took me for
My sister and was angry – only in
The morning. Waking, he bent over me
To speak, turned white with shock and horror,
Rushed like twenty madmen from the tent,
Shouting Laban's name. Laban, safe
Behind a barrier of servants armed
With staves, came slily up and, in a lull
In Jacob's storm: 'Another seven years

For Rachel,' he said quietly. 'Agree –
And you can marry her next week – but *first*
You are to serve your week with Leah.'

DINAH (*ironically*) A practical man!

LEAH And for that moment of discovery I've
Done penance all my life – and so have all
My sons, the offspring of the unwanted, lesser bride –
With two sons each from Bilhah and from Zilpah,
Jacob's concubines. Continually we've
Been slighted. As I bore each son, his name
Expressed my hope to please my husband, or
My gratitude to God for hearing me.
Pointless to name my third son 'Levi'. I
And Jacob never were 'United'. Once,
With Reuben's present to me of mandragora,
I bought him from my sister for the night.
I stooped so low! Now – Jacob's worship of
His Rachel's boy inflames the jealousy
Of ten grown men. My earlier, bitter envy is
My sons' inheritance.

DINAH Entirely true.
When Rachel died, my father Jacob put
A second idol in her shrine, her son,
Her first born, Joseph. Wasn't it foreseeable?

LEAH (*in despair*) Too much, too much for all his other sons
To bear! A month ago, one son alone,
The second youngest son, was given a splendid
robe,
The others – nothing. Secretly they seethed.
Even Judah paled in anger and dismay
At such lop-sided generosity.

My husband should show equal love. It is
Morality to treat all members of
One family alike, if you are Patriarch
And head of all the clan.

DINAH Certainly
It's *vexing*, but not tragic. (*She stands up.*)

LEAH In this cauldron of
Embittered lives, what may not happen, as men rage?
Perhaps the tragedy is still to come.
(*in frustration*) I'm weary of the pattern of my life,
Disheartened by the never-ending toil!

DINAH The life is hard in our encampment close to Hebron.
Inhabiting this valley in our goatskin tents,
We think like nomads and have never placed
One course of mudbricks on another. With
So many animals to graze, how can
We settle? But we women stay here, while
In ever wider arcs our shepherds strike
Out from the camp for richer pasturage.
We women labour all our waking hours
With fires, pots, ovens, brushes, distaffs, looms –
And sow our scanty plots of emmer wheat.
Where is there visual beauty in our lives?
In bartered artefacts – a little pottery,
Some ornamental pins for women's hair.
The landscape of our lives is rocks and dust,
With tufts of green to feed the herds. There
Are richer lives.

LEAH (*firmly*) Jacob is the owner of
Substantial property.

DINAH Our way of life
Is fixed. Wealth makes no difference to us.
So, Leah, I'll draw more water from the well.
(stands up)
But here they come. Our shepherds have come home.

LEAH Look, Dinah, look. Fetch Jacob, quickly now.
(Exit Dinah)
They've nearly reached the camp. Now *why* would they
Be moving side by side so slowly down
The slope, wide gaps between them, grimly staring,
Like lonely men advancing to their deaths.
This is ominous.

Enter Jacob and Dinah out of breath as Joseph's brothers begin to assemble. Jacob, Leah and Dinah stare at them in dismay.

Something terrible . . .

Judah, standing with Simeon, Levi, Dan, begins to speak as the other five enter, Naphtali, Gad. Asher, Issachar and Zebulun.

JUDAH (*wearily*) My father Jacob – I have evil news.

JACOB (*surprised*) Where's Joseph? Why not send him here to bring
Me word, as we arranged. Why, Judah? Why
Return? My boy, where is he? Where are all
The herds? They're healthy?

JUDAH Reuben guards them on
The farther slope, but as for Joseph, (*griefstricken*) Jacob,
We wonder, could this be his robe? The boy
Has vanished.

JACOB (*numbed*) Let me look. What can this mean?
Dried lakes of blood, rents and gashes as if
A wild beast's claws had ripped it. Yes – this is
His robe. It's Joseph's. Poor soul. What do you suppose . . . ?

JUDAH We fear that Joseph has been mauled to death.
This tattered robe, all blood-drenched as you see
It now, we found at Dothan.

JACOB (*utters a sob, then speaks with quiet firmness*) No, my son's
Not dead. There's no real proof, no body.

JUDAH (*in a dead voice*) Look!

JACOB (*in quiet despair*) My Joseph. Oh my son, your garment tells
The story of an ugly, futile death.
The agony is larger than my life.
The human breast cannot endure it. I am
A grain of sand within a tidal wave
Of pain.(*he falters*) My Joseph, seventeen years old.
(*more firmly*) My head is crowned with sorrows till I die.

LEAH The poor boy! Eaten by a beast! That was
The tragedy I sensed. Joseph's spirit, as

He saw a monstrous death approaching,
Cried out to me for help and, after he
Had lost his life, like a smoky pall
His fear hung in the air, hovering over all
The land from Dothan down to Hebron. My dear son! (*a sob*)

DINAH (*with passion*) Inexplicable God! What purpose can
Such sorrow serve? I thought our life was full
Enough of useless deaths, brimful, a cistern full
Of corpses, full of blood, with dead men sprawling round
The rim – and yet there had to be one more! (*reflectively*)
What a youth you were – the only male to
Offer me respect since Shechem's death. (*in agony*) Joseph!

JACOB How shall a man live who has lost his son
And finds his life too long? My tears will fill
A Great Green Sea of grief, in which I'll drown –
No foothold in the dreary depths, no shore
Of hope to reach. Though my body may live on,
My heart is dead.

JUDAH (*in a low voice*) Simeon, what have we done?

JACOB Did God make such a lad, to let him die before
He reached full manhood? This makes no sense to me.

JUDAH (*in a low voice*) Simeon, this is how he would have mourned
The death of any of his sons.

SIMEON (*in a low voice*) Wait, Judah, wait!

JACOB My adoration should have shielded my
Dear son from death. So little power – from so
Much love! And did I ever show you how
I loved you? So much love – and left unsaid,
Unguessed. I was too harsh; trying to
Teach discipline to what my soul adored.
And I must spend the rest of life without
Your presence to delight me. Joseph, Joseph!

SIMEON (*in a low voice*) Maudlin ramblings, Judah! There'll be worse!

JACOB I have lost my Joseph, first born of my princess,
Of my dearest Rachel. Often I would say
To him: 'You are my spiritual heir.
You have been singled out by God, as in
My generation he chose me, in spite
Of my ambition and duplicity.
We are a chosen tribe, predestined, set
To travel the exceptional road of faith,
Proclaiming on this earth the one true God,
The giant God, to whom Mount Sinai's
A jagged pebble; God, who promised to
My ancestor, to Abraham, descendants
Numerous as grains of sand, or stars in heaven.'
(*powerfully*) Now my faith in Israel's destiny is shaken.
A wild animal has killed the light.
I press your bloodstained garment to my lips,
And kiss the suffering blood of my dear son.
(*softly*) No solace. Desolation. Desolation.
No solace anywhere!

JUDAH (*softly*) You heard that, Simeon?
We‘re *nothing* to our father. My heart is dark
Again and pitiless!

JACOB I feel such horror!
And I repent again of all my sins,
The sins I know of, and the sins of which
I am not, and may never be aware.
Now that my soul is ill with grief, how fervently
I wish that I had been a better man.
Yet God forgave me all my sins, and blessed
Me when I wrestled with him all night long
At Penuel. Next day my brother Esau –
My brother whom I'd cheated of his birthright and
His blessing from our dying father Isaac –
Esau, with four hundred men, forgave me too.
So God and man forgave, but I abhor myself!
I am ill. I am all grief. My son has gone.

JUDAH (*coldly*) What preparation, father, shall we make
For mourning our young brother Joseph?

JACOB (*controlled*) I am at fault, my sons, forgetting I
am not
The only mourner of my slaughtered son.
The loss is cruel to us all. Forgive me.
We must mourn a life which was a great
Achievement. Joseph's was a life of truth,
Unswerving in reliability.
To be a mortal who may be depended on
May seem small and yet it is enormous.
My sons, I know how you will miss his power,
The blessed emanation of his soul,
His generosity and sympathy

And humour. We shall mourn him; we will shave
Away one side of all our beards and of
The hair on all our heads, wear prickly cloth
That irritates the skin, pour wood ash from
The fire over faces streaked with tears.
Once more I kiss the clothing my son wore
When his poor body suffered. (*a sob*)
The youth is dead and we shall never see
The glory of the man. God of Bethel,
Help me. Help this miserable speck of dust!

ACT I

THE STEWARD

SCENE I

Avaris, Hyksos capital of Egypt, in the Nile delta. The house of Potiphar, captain of Pharaoh's palace guard. The chief reception room, with walls painted with scenes of the Nile, including animals and birds, with no visible windows (they are clerestory) and with two pillars set towards the front of the stage which divide the width of the stage into three equal parts. The pillars are painted and have carved capitals ressembling clusters of palm leaves, Someone in a distant room plays a brief melody on a harp. Enter Potiphar and Seneb.

POTIPHAR (*heartily*) Yes, come indoors, come indoors! Good
To see you after your year away! Seneb,
I congratulate you on your victory.

SENEB So did the Occupier of Egypt's Throne.
On pain of death we may not touch the king,
Yet, as I fell prostrate on the ground,
His majesty instructed me to kiss his foot.

POTIPHAR Seneb, your career is made! We've
A party on the tenth day of this week.
Join us, and be welcomed home in style.

SENEB Delighted, Potiphar. And what's your news?

POTIPHAR Nothing's changed. I'm captain of the palace guard still,
Living in the aura of his majesty, the god.

SENEB And busy about your villa and estate, no doubt.
They seem in splendid shape.

POTIPHAR My Hebrew slave
Attends to them. I bought him in the market here
When he was seventeen. First he was
A household servant, then my valet. Finding him
Honest, generous-minded and immensely
Capable, I've made him steward over all
I own. He's loved by all the gods. Everything
He touches prospers.

SENEB (*musingly*) Hm. I can't call him to mind.

POTIPHAR He seems like an Egyptian, with his round
Black poll, his eyes outlined in malachite,
His faultless accent and calligraphy –
Note this! – writing worthy of a House of Life!

SENEB He reads and writes? Surprising. The Hebrews, like
Our Bedouin marauders, have fierce and craggy
Principles and eagle noses. Emphatically,
They never read or write. Would pillage be
The only occupation of his tribe?

POTIPHAR They are shepherds.

SENEB Ah! Pillage is secondary!

POTIPHAR I'll not hide from you that Joseph's here
Because his jealous brothers sold him as a slave.

SENEB Primitive! Horrific! Just like the Bedouin. (*laughs*)

POTIPHAR (*gruffly*) My slave returns the compliment. 'You worship
Several gods,' he says. 'That's backward!'

SENEB (*laughs*) Not several. Hundreds!

POTIPHAR 'There's only one,'
He tells me patiently. 'You give him many names,
Duplicating or dividing up his attributes.'

SENEB Could a foreigner understand our gods?
And look who's putting us right – a man from a tent!
Laughable! Backward? Look at our buildings, our canals,
Our trade, our literature – our ancient monuments,
The superhuman pyramids of Gizeh,
Giant jewels glittering and blazing in
The sun! Our ancient civilization backward? (*laughs*)
What does a man in a tent achieve? His food supply!
Coming here, your Hebrew made a cultural leap
Of two millennia!

POTIPHAR (*thoughtfully*) Perhaps he didn't say 'backward'.

SENEB Hm. How can it matter what a servant thinks?

POTIPHAR Which reminds me – I can't bring my wife Anhai
To treat him with respect. She keeps on ordering him

To take a lunch of bread and beer and find
Her nephew at the temple school! If I tell
Anhai that isn't what my steward's for,
A tempest swirls about my head.

SENEB How is Anhai?

POTIPHAR Thank you, she's well, she's very well. Ah,
My beautiful enigma! I never know
When she will take offence, nor why I'm
suddenly
Restored to favour. She'll come upon me in
Her finest wig, give me a sultry sidelong look
And say the omens are propitious when I least
Expect it. My lithe and graceful leopard is
An enchantress like the goddess Isis!

SENEB No other women can compare with our
Luxuriant Egyptian beauties. My wife and I'll
Look forward to your party. If you'll excuse
Me now, I've business at the ministry.

POTIPHAR I'll escort you to the gate.

Exeunt Potiphar and Seneb. Enter Simonides.

SIMONIDES (*comically*) I thought those two would never go.
They've been keeping me from my work!
(*conversationally*) If a friend had said to me when I
was young: 'Simonides, guess where you'll be at
forty,' what would I have answered?
'Easy! I shall be a slave in the Egyptian Capital
Avaris on the south side of our Great Green Sea?'
– No way!

But here I am, slaving away for the Sun-baked Race, here in Egypt, tarting up my master's house for a party.
I was on a vessel crossing to Phoenicia, when a pirate galley rammed it in time-honoured style.
Farewell liberty and homeland, wife and child!
Farewell to the merchant who employed me. He was killed.
Hm. The painted walls all round me need a little touching up. (*tracing a pattern as he faces the audience*) Here in front of me the paint is flaking from a pintail's wings. There it goes, flying over the papyrus umbels in this beautiful depiction of our delta marshland. – Then there are the palm tree pillars. Someone, cobra, cat or drunk Egyptian lady's taken bites out – here.
I must get some plaster, sometime.

POTIPHAR (*off*) Simonides!

SIMONIDES Be quiet!
A cushy number, this was, till our master thought of making Joseph steward. Till then the garden had a stagnant pond and we a cobwebbed life of slothful comfort.
(*dryly*) Joseph's an enthusiast.
Working for him – goes against the grain.
He should rule an empire!
(*conversationally*) Yes, now we are as frenetic as locusts all day long. Everything shines and sparkles, like the eyes of Potiphar's wife Anhai, as they gloat on Joseph's person. What an inflammatory situation we have here! I have heard

her offering herself to him. He refused her – most politely. It was a fascinating scene! Hm. Affection and respect bind Potiphar and Hebrew Joseph, while Potiphar is blind to all the failings of Anhai.

POTIPHAR (*off, crossly*) Simonides!

SIMONIDES (*with tremendous zeal*) Coming my lord! Coming in two shakes of a sistrum!
Every slave is harried and chivvied from morning to night.

Exit Simonides.

SCENE II

The same. The lamplit room is crowded and abuzz with conversation. At the bidding of Joseph and Simonides, servants move among the guests filling goblets from wine jars. Harp music may be heard from time to time. Potiphar and Seneb each speak to several people while Anhai is conversing with Seneb's wife, Kiya.

POTIPHAR (*raising his cup*) Drink up, my guests! Enjoy the pleasures of the evening! Life, health, prosperity to all!

KIYA What delicious meat and fruit, Anhai! Now I shall inhale the scent of my blue lotus in a golden haze of wine.

ANHAI Ah, Kiya. You'll be proud of all your husband's feats of derring-do! We *admire* Seneb.
Talking of gold, I've lost a figurine, a cat, in bronze, with golden eyes. Joseph, look for it until you find it!

POTIPHAR Anhai, Anhai! Joseph, send the Syrian servant girl instead. You forget, Anhai. Joseph's grown to manhood.

KIYA My son mislaid his crocodile. Such a hullabaloo! Seizing the Horus lock on the side of his head, I tugged it hard to shut him up. – You know,
Anhai – the wooden crocodile with movable
jaws . . .

ANHAI Yes, Kiya, jaws that open and shut. The other day we lost a laundryman. Imagine him forgetting to look out for floating logs! Only his jar of lupin powder and a pile of oily linen showed where he had been!

KIYA (*sensibly*) Lupin powder cleans *so well*.. (*musingly*) I wonder, am I right to give my child a crocodile as a toy?

POTIPHAR Amazing instinct of the mother crocs – in those dreadful jaws they carry batches of their new-hatched young and place them gently in the Nile.

SENEB Hippopotami are worse than crocodiles. They'll bite a boat in half, let alone a man!

POTIPHAR All the fun of the hunt! And I like to see their tiny whirring ears and pink-lined nostrils rising from the flowers in the river.

SENEB Extremely nasty entering hippopotamus territory on land – marked out by hillocks of new dung.

SIMONIDES (*aside, ironically*) Hark at them! Why worry here about an extra odour? The Nile valley always stinks of fish and fowl.
Wealthy folk buy perfumed oil and incense as a counterblast.
Each lady at this party's crowned with wax – a cone of scented wax which cools her as it melts in rivulets.
Maddening to servants sliding in the ointment!
If this were my house I would not invite this rabble!

ANHAI (*softly*) Joseph! Joseph, I love you

JOSEPH (*with quiet urgency*) Anhai, remember where and who you are!

ANHAI When you last drank beer, you drank with it a spell I bought to make you love me – written on the ostracon inside the pot. I paid a sorcerer to write it.

JOSEPH (*calmly*) Think of your husband and your guests.

ANHAI I've recited spells to make me irresistible to you!

JOSEPH (*dryly, impassively*) If you were the goddess of my life, I could not take you.

ANHAI I'm wearing amulets to shield our love affair from all the hostile dead.

JOSEPH (*softly*) I'm your husband's faithful servant.
(*in a ringing voice*) Yes, my lady! *(claps his hands; to servant)*
Three more jars of Delta wine. At once!

POTIPHAR Seneb, look! The man who's calmly turning from Anhai – that's the steward. He is all I said and more. The gods sent boyhood dreams to him in which his family, sun, moon and stars, bowed down to him.

SENEB Well they might! I'm sure his tribe of Canaanites would find him most impressive. He's dignified.
You say he has improved your land – better irrigation, vegetable gardens, granaries and so forth – working tirelessly. May I ask your steward a question?

POTIPHAR By all means. (*loudly*) Joseph! Seneb has a query.

SENEB You appear unusually serene. What is your secret?

JOSEPH (*slowly*) My lord, a wise Egyptian said that 'What the god commands is that which happens. Live in the midst of quiet. What the gods will give comes of itself'.

SENEB Bravo, young man!
And Potiphar, your Hebrew has survived the culture shock!
Quoting Ptahhotep, no less, 'The Wisdom of'.
Thank heaven I'm back in civilised society!

POTIPHAR (*with enthusiasm*) What's more, you are the hero of the hour!

SENEB (*briskly*) I was lucky. My best scout gave timely warning of a larger army lying in wait below a ridge to steal the tin we'd mined. We pretended to attempt a pincer movement to enclose the enemy, but let them gallop through our centre to the baggage train we'd left unguarded. Half stopped to loot, as we had hoped, splitting their forces. (*proudly*) The rest is history.

ANHAI (*mischievously*) You weren't afraid to leave your wife so many months alone?

KIYA (*reproachfully*) Anhai!

SENEB (*laughs*) She adores me, don't you, Kiya? Also she's religious.
Ra's all-seeing eye would keep her honest!
(*theatrically, flippantly, commanding everyone's attention)* Listen to my cautionary tale!
Let's suppose a lady – call her 'Tubu' – has been guilty of undetected adultery. She dies, is called to judgment and must stand beside Anubis god of death to watch the weighing of her heart. Wise Thoth, ibis-headed, also stands beside the scales to write the verdict in his register.

SEVERAL PEOPLE (*in awe*) Ah!

ANHAI (*frivously, musically*) You're frightening us, Seneb.

JOSEPH (*aside*) Anhai doesn't think of *worldly* consequences, never mind eternal.

SENEB (*with brisk gaiety*) Tubu stands on one side. On the other crouches Amemet. the great Devourer, a crocodile with lion's abdomen and belly, hippopotamus hind-quarters.
Slavering, he looks at Tubu. (*with relish*) Is she for him?

SEVERAL PEOPLE (*in awe*) Ah!

SENEB Tubu's heart's being weighed against the ostrich feather of the truth. Ma'at the feather settles softly, vertically, in the right hand pan. Anubis holds above the left the heart of Tubu. With his human hand the jackal gently lowers the heart and leaves it in the pan. A terrible silence falls!

SEVERAL PEOPLE (*in awe*) Ah!

SENEB 'A pity,' says great Osiris on his throne – from which the Crystal river flows. He sighs. 'To quote the poet: "The lady is as lovely as date bread dipped in beer", but she is not victorious, not justified. Her voice is not the voice of truth.'
Forty-two judges heave a gusty sigh, blowing Ma'at the feather (*laughs*) – heaven knows where!
'I'll write down: "Failed",' says Thoth. 'No cakes and ale for the lady. She'll not "come forth by day" to eternal bliss.'
Anubis says: 'The monster gets the lady'.

'Oh my little mandragora berry!' cries the monster, in delight, scrunching as the lady screeches.
(*triumphantly*) There's my moral tale!

There is a little nervous laughter as general conversation resumes.

POTIPHAR (*gravely*) I am astonished at your levity, good friend – a soul lost for the After-Life, a sinful heart eaten by the monster – and you *laugh.*
Man's Judgment by the gods is a most sacred and most solemn mystery.

SENEB (*comically*) Heavens! I've not commissioned any!

KIYA Any what?

SENEB Scenes of love life for our funerary chapel.

KIYA Hurry, Seneb, or we'll have to do without for all eternity!

POTIPHAR (*seriously*) An erotic ambience is quite enough. It isn't necessary to be explicit. Show Kiya playing a harp or sistrum on a bed, beside her a blue lotus in an alabaster vase.

KIYA Sweet-scented is my love,
A fragrant lotus flower;
We shall each other love
Within the garden bower.

Within the Western land
Where Egypt is reborn

We'll saunter hand in hand
Beneath eternal sun.

POTIPHAR Very good, Kiya. That would make a nice tomb text.

KIYA I'm sure the After-Life will be a party in celestial Egypt.

SENEB Potiphar, thank you. It has been delightful.

POTIPHAR Goodnight, my friends.

SEVERAL PEOPLE Delightful! Thank you. We'll take our leave. Goodnight.

SENEB Life, health, happiness to you and all our thanks.

SCENE III

The same. Enter Joseph rapidly with a hunted air. Enter Anhai with violent energy.

ANHAI (*pleadingly*) My love! Joseph, listen to me!

JOSEPH (*with quiet urgency*) Keep your voice down!

ANHAI (*fairly loudly*) I am like Egypt's captives, elbows tied
Above their heads. Do what you will with me!

JOSEPH (*almost as loudly*) I will do nothing! He bought me as a slave,
Yet Potiphar has given me everything he owns,
Everything but you. For heaven's sake, avoid me!

ANHAI (*with intensity*) To say no to me is not the slightest use.
I shall persist until you eat!

JOSEPH (*stonily*) You have
My body in your bed whenever Potiphar
Is with you. There is one male body, which you have.

ANHAI (*angrily*) What *do* you mean! What nonsense!

JOSEPH (*with authority, but a little breathlessly*) Think, Anhai!
Physical man you know entirely,
Caressing and receiving him in perfect honour.
All I have to offer is the same
Sensation, plus the very transitory thrill
Of your awareness of the presence of
A different personality. It isn't worth
Betraying for! It's not worth dying for! Leave me
Alone, Anhai! You don't *need* me!

ANHAI I'll
Pay any price! I'm dying of my love for you!

JOSEPH A passing whim! You have your husband's and
My company – no threat of losing either. Leave
It be! You'd gain nothing – loose sand slipping through
Your fingers, making quicksands for our lives!
You are Eve desiring Adam. You

Desire your husband, lady. Invite him to
Your bed more often!

ANHAI (*aside*) Such unmanly behaviour!
I must be mad – bewitched. If he were worth
His salt, he'd need no more encouragement.
He'd *drag* me into bed – with some pretence
Of force!(*to Joseph, angrily*)You chide me like a backward child.
You sound just like a scribe. Show more respect!

JOSEPH (*firmly*) *Less* respect is what you want from me,
But I'll not offer less. Your husband owns
Me, yet he treats me as an equal. You
Are his. You're *sacrosanct*!

ANHAI Coward's talk!

JOSEPH (*aside*) Disastrous! Impossible to reason with her.

ANHAI Be bold! Claim what you want! I'll force you to!

She seizes him in her arms. They wrestle.

JOSEPH I am – stronger than you – in every way.

ANHAI How, in every way?

Joseph succeeds in breaking free and steps back. Anhai makes no further attempt to close with him.

JOSEPH (*breathlessly*) Physically – also
Through obedience to God. I've
Decided absolutely – what I will not do.

ANHAI (*scornfully*) Cant! Humbug! Take what you want. Do
As you wish! Acknowledge your own greatness!

JOSEPH (*briskly*) That would be a sad delusion.

ANHAI (*furiously*) You – you hypocrite!

JOSEPH (*extending his arms pleadingly*) I'm an ordinary man, trying to
Prevent disaster.

ANHAI I don't care what happens.
I will have my way!

JOSEPH (*emphatically*) Potiphar
Is worth fidelity. He is a man
Of rectitude. Learn from his excellence.

ANHAI (*swiftly*) It is a very boring excellence.
I am looking for excitement, for adventure.

JOSEPH (*flatly*) Ah well, I'm very boring too. Any
Excitation would be strictly temporary.

ANHAI (*wildly*) What hostile demon has inspired in me
This passion for a man pretending to
Be made of stone, aloof, superior,
A very Pharaoh, perching on a pyramid
And pelting me with precepts! I know what lies
Beneath. You're passionate; and what I am
Appeals to you. There must be some way I
Can tempt you to admit it. Oh! Your austere
Resistance galls me. One day I'll be
Revenged. You shall burn with passion just

As I do now and I shall free myself
And gloat to see you suffer. Or else, I swear,
If you'll not burn with love for me, you'll burn
With hate! You have tormented me enough!
You underestimate a great Egyptian lady!

Exit Anhai.

JOSEPH (*soberly*) I am afraid. Anhai's a furnace capable
Of burning all my future. I thought my self-control
Would save us both, but now I see, refusing her,
I still may come to grief. One hope remains.
Soon, by invitation of the king
She'll join the royal barge and sail to Thebes
With Potiphar. Anhai's *regard* for me
May cool as she receives the compliments
Of scented Theban nobles. When she travels I'll
Be free of persecution and temptation –
For a while, at least.

Exit Joseph.

SCENE IV

The same. Enter Simonides.

SIMONIDES (*solemnly*) You would expect a slave from Greece
to rise
Above Egyptian superstitions, but I can't.
There is an *atmosphere* today. The lion
Gargoyles on the roof are no protection from

The evil in the rain. I can feel
Malignant spirits, crowding round the villa,
Peering in clerestory windows. Evil is
Swirling through the house. Anhai is
Possessed, as dangerous as a lioness.
With feral eyes, she watches Joseph's every move.
Pale and ill, to inspire jealousy,
She twines her arms about her husband in
The steward's presence. Hopeless desire dashes itself
Against unyielding rock. Joseph has
Departed from inscrutability.
Despairingly he shakes his head, like one who says:
'No good can come of this.' (*sourly*) It's no use
asking me
To pity him. My soul's been cauterised
By personal loss. I regard all human
Antics, so predictable, as comical –
A very sour joke. When it's time
For Joseph's slaughter, what'll I do? – Fold
My arms, philosophising: 'Such is life.'
He has just returned to the empty house.
I believe this afternoon Anhai is at
The villa of some friends . . .

JOSEPH (*off*) Leave me alone!

SIMONIDES No, she isn't! Here comes Joseph, running, and
The lady after. Time for me to disappear.
Witnesses will be unpopular.

Exit Simonides. Enter Joseph, pursued by Anhai.

ANHAI (*breathlessly, wildly*) I warn you, Joseph! Time is
running out!

JOSEPH (*vehemently*) Leave me alone! Go away!

ANHAI Through the north
Porch I see servants coming though the gate.
In spite of all you've said I know that you
Desire me. Promise you will sleep with me
When next there is an opportunity!

JOSEPH (*vigorously*) I never will!

ANHAI (*in a frenzy*) That was your last chance!

Joseph cries out in alarm as she tears at his cloak.

ANHAI There! I've ripped your cloak from you, torn
It from your shoulders. This is the evidence –
The evidence of your assault on me, of your
Indecency. Now I'll tell Potiphar
You tried to force me. I shall turn you over to
My husband's rage. Just watch me!

Exit Joseph. Anhai begins to pursue him, but she quickly comes to a halt.

ANHAI (*breathlessly*) That's right! Run
And try to prove you were elsewhere, you Hebrew!
You
Will only look the guiltier. Your life is over!
Help, servants! Save me! Seize the steward!
(*She screams*)

Enter servants.

1ST SERVANT What is the matter, mistress?

ANHAI Seize the foreign steward! Don't let him escape!

Exeunt servants.

VOICES (*off*) He's doubling back! Cut him off! He's cornered!

Enter servants, dragging Joseph.

ANHAI (*shuddering*) Hold him tightly! Keep that monster from me!

1ST SERVANT Here comes Potiphar, with giant strides.

Enter Potiphar.

ANHAI (*imploringly*) My husband, give me justice!

POTIPHAR (*angrily*) By all the gods
Of Egypt, what is this?

ANHAI This – this *man* attacked me!

POTIPHAR (*thunderously*) Which man, Anhai? Not Joseph!

ANHAI (*tragically*) Never use
The traitor's name! Destroy his name! Kill
The man and throw him in the Nile! This 'no name'
Assaulted me when I was here alone!
He laid his lecherous hands on me and tried . . .
Potiphar, my husband, hold me – keep me safe!

POTIPHAR Joseph, you . . . You have dared . . . After all
The honourable thoughts you have professed,
You could give in to common lust! I

Am disappointed in you to the point
Of heartbreak. (*sadly*) Some folk wear a mask a
Simple man like me can never guess at.

ANHAI (*with the hint of a tear*) I was in my bedroom, sorting through
A chest of clothes. That man appeared before
My eyes as suddenly as grasses in
The desert after rain. Closing the chest,
I asked him what he wanted. (*with hurt astonishment*) Coolly he
Explained his purpose, asking for co-operation.

POTIPHAR Infamous!

ANHAI Outraged, I attempted to
Run past him – but with iron arms he caught
Me to his breast. I – shrieked with fright.

POTIPHAR Anhai,
Did he succeed? Oh, this is unendurable!

ANHAI (*after a tiny sob, bravely*) He teased me, let me almost free myself,
Studying me with lascivious, laughing eyes.
I was a bird trapped in his net. When
His playful hold was weaker, suddenly
I tore myself away and ran out, crying out
For help – but no help came.

POTIPHAR I shall strangle him!
How can I restrain myself?

ANHAI (*breathlessly*) Your Hebrew caught

Me here – flung me down and fell on me,
Gruffly promising himself the pleasures he
Had longed for. Desperately I struggled, though
Nearly faint with horror; screamed, without hope.
(*changing tone*)
I thank the gods the servants came in time.

POTIPHAR Horrible, horrible! Joseph, I cannot
Believe that you are so depraved. I gave
You everything I had, everything except
Anhai, and it was not enough for you!

ANHAI (*like a somnambulist coming to*) I seem
To have his cloak here in my hand. How did
It get there? Here is the evidence. I must
Have torn it from him as we wrestled. See
How hard I tried to prevent – his invasion
Of the body that belongs to you!
Look at him – horror-struck, tongue-tied with guilt!
Now you see the value of the man
You made all-powerful!

POTIPHAR (*in agony*) Never was I
So deceived and disappointed in another
Human being! This – makes me despair
Of all mankind. Speak to me, Joseph! Speak
Nameless one!

JOSEPH (*in desperation*) I am innocent, I swear
To God! I am innocent!

POTIPHAR (*wrathfully*) Is my wife a liar?

JOSEPH Your wife is feverishly ill!

POTIPHAR (*savagely*) Take him!
Take this criminal away before I kill him.
My poor wife's tears should make him beg
forgiveness
On his knees. Instead, he tells brazen lies.
He feels no remorse! Since he is so anxious to
Lie down, take him to the courtyard. Thrash him
With tamarisk rods. Pharaoh's jail shall keep
This smooth young rogue away from women till
He dies! Lead him away.

Exeunt servants with Joseph.

POTIPHAR (*to Anhai, tenderly*) My dearest love, I am deeply
sorry.
I was wrong to trust a foreign slave.

ANHAI (*calmly*) You are not to blame. He looks innocence
Personified.

POTIPHAR (*Aside, in agony*) Joseph! I loved you once.
Joseph! (*loudly*) I must supervise the beating in
The garden. The wretch shall keep his life. Rest
In your room, my poor Anhai! (*Aside*) How could such
A man be evil? I would have staked my *life*
On his integrity. In all the mists
Of rage my heart is sore for him.

Exit Potiphar. Off-stage a rod swishes in slow cadence.

ANHAI (*amazed*) Who is that man? Who is the Hebrew?
I have just destroyed him. He staggered out,
Between two furious servants who manhandled him,
To immediate torture and the lifelong

Twilight of a prison, all because I lied
About him in my passion. His eyes met mine.
What did I read in them? Not hate. Not anger.
Pity! He cast on me a look of weary pity. *(angrily)*
He pitied *me*. He *dared* to pity *me*. *(sound of blows,off)*
Yes, *beat* him! *(in exasperation)* Why did you refuse me, Joseph?
Never would you have known such love-making!
(*she listens*) I hear the green rods cutting welts into
His wounded back. Instead of these avenging blows
He might have had thousands of libidinous
Caresses . . . (*feverishly*) I will not melt with carnal
Adoration. The fool! He should have *listened.*
What's for him now? A wasted life. A death in prison.

Exit Anhai, to the continuing sound of blows. At last there comes a cry of agony.

ACT II

THE VIZIER

SCENE I

Pharaoh's prison in Avaris. A corridor giving on to a cell. The cell contains a water jar on a stand and one stool. Pharaoh's butler sits on the stool and Pharaoh's baker, some distance away from him, on the floor. Enter the Captain of the prison, followed by Joseph carrying keys and a bowl of food.

CAPTAIN (*briskly*) You are blest by all seven Hathors, Joseph.
In all the years you've spent here in my prison,
Your labours have lightened the burden of
My duties and responsibilities. Because
God smiles on you, your presence blesses us.

JOSEPH (*mildly*) I'm glad to be of service.

CAPTAIN (*surprised*) Joseph, look!
Look here! The royal baker and his friend the butler –
Through the grating you can see them slumped in misery.
Remind me.What was their offence again?

JOSEPH Aiding and abetting thieves, who purloined
Storage jars from palace warehouses.

CAPTAIN A foolish act. A fool isn't necessarily
A rogue, but every rogue's a fool.

JOSEPH They look afraid.

CAPTAIN Question them. See me later.

Exit Captain as Joseph unlocks the gate, enters the cell and sets the bowl of food down on the floor.

JOSEPH I've brought your meal. You look in need of help.

BAKER (*mesmerised*) Dreams haunt us, ghostly dreams, the terror of
The soul.

JOSEPH Dreams? I can interpret dreams,
God willing.

BAKER Ah! It would be best to know
Their meaning.

BUTLER Very well. As royal butler I
Am senior. In my dream I saw a three
Branched grapevine, stick-like, then in bud, in leaf,
In blossom; petals fell, seed-cases swelled.
I picked ripe grapes and squeezed. I saw juice foaming in
The royal goblet in my hand. I gave
It to the king.

JOSEPH (*briskly*) Three branches signify
Three days of waiting for your pardon from the king,
Whose wine you'll serve that day. (*urgently*) Remember me,
The Hebrew, Joseph, torn from my family
In Canaan, sold as a slave, falsely charged
And held in Pharaoh's prison. Ask the king
To free me!

BUTLER I will, I will! Restored to favour!

BAKER (*joyfully leaping up*) And my dream, Joseph? On my head I bore
Three baker's baskets. In the topmost I
Saw honey breads and other Royal favourites. Birds
Came swooping from the sky to peck the cakes.
I saw each feather of their spreading wings.

JOSEPH (*sadly*) I'm sorry, friend. The baskets mean three days.
In three days you'll be executed.

BAKER (*after a groan*) I see.
My headless body, hanging in the air,
Will feed the vultures, kites and crows.

JOSEPH Prepare
Yourself to meet your gods.

BAKER Ra, the heart of Ptah,
Who prompted Ptah to utter World-Creating words
With Thoth, his tongue. I shall implore their mercy.
What's the use? My soul must die the double death.
I'll never see the glory of the gods.

BUTLER Such wonderful news!

JOSEPH (*dryly*) Your cell-mate is to die.

BUTLER (*cheerfully*) That *is* a shame! The god of Egypt is
Inspired to pardon me. I'll pour his wine!

JOSEPH And when you do, remember the interpreter
Of dreams. Tell Pharaoh I am innocent.

BUTLER Of course. The splendour of the turquoise and
The gold! Three days – and I shall see it!

BAKER Gladly I
Would wait three years to see my executioner.

JOSEPH I'll see you later. Pray. (*to himself*) Poor man,
poor man!

Joseph leaves the cell and locks it. He takes a few slow steps and comes to a halt.

JOSEPH (*simply*) That feckless sommelier will tell the king
I'm innocent. – So this has been a four
Year prison sentence. God knows vanity
And arrogance have been thrashed out of me
Too often and too long! Is it a privilege
To be chastened? Does it serve a purpose?
I've always had strong limbs and all my faculties,
Food, clothing, air to breathe, a place to sleep;
Sudden pain, and mortal fear, were brief.
Yet there is no depth of human misery
I have not sounded. Agony of soul,
Twice seizing me, has lacerated me.

In the night-time I would wrestle with
The angel of my sorrows. How often
Did I crouch, on sand or beaten earth,
Arms tightly folded round my chest, rocking back
And forth with silent screams, as torrents of
Tempestuous tears flowed down my cheeks
And trickled in the fabric at my neck.
By day – by day I practised discipline,
Endeavouring as a slave to be the best
Of slaves, to trust the purposes of God
And do my utmost. *Twice* – I have been hurled
From precipices into wells of shame and grief.
Twice I've taught myself serenity.
When I was a boy, the God of Abraham
And Israel sent me dreams of an
Illustrious future. To be *free* will be *enough.*
When the waters of the flood recede,
I'll be content to sow the crop and watch
The pigs that trample in the seed. Blithely I
Shall scythe the ripened wheat, then quaff my beer
While eating bread and onions in the shade.
(*joyfully*) In a week, or in a month, I shall be
free! (*Exit*)

SCENE II

Pharaoh's Hall of Audience in the palace at Avaris. Pillars support the roof. There is a golden throne on a dais. The hall is thronged with officials, petitioners, emissaries, guards. The butler is conspicuous among them. He remains isolated and shows signs of desperate anxiety. A trumpet fanfare causes the crowd to fall silent and draw back to either side, so that a wide approach way leads to the throne. Enter Ushers carrying golden rods, Pharaoh and two well-dressed Fan-bearers carrying long-stemmed fans, each consisting of several large ostrich plumes. Coming to a halt the ushers strike the floor once with their rods.

USHERS Tremble, the god is coming!
(strike the floor once) Tremble, the god is coming!
(strike the floor once) Tremble, the god is coming!

ALL IN CHORUS Life to his majesty, prosperity and health!
Life to his majesty, prosperity and health!

KHYAN (*majestically*) I am Egypt's god-king, Egypt's Pontifex,
Her bridge to the immortal gods. I
Am Ra. I am the River Nile. I
Am Barley; and I am Osiris.
Unless seed dies and earth receives it, there
Will be no barley harvest, nor Osirian
Rebirth of mortal man. While I live,
By daily ritual and chant, I,
And all who serve the gods on my behalf,
Preserve the ordered harmony of Egypt,
Shielding her from Chaos which, unquiet,
Hissing with menacing murmurings and mutterings,
Waits to burst in and claw us to destruction.
Even though our sacred rites protect us –
Two threatening portents have appeared – dreams
Which Syrian sorcerers have fathomed and
Will now explain.

A Syrian steps foward and prostrates himself before the king. At a gesture from the king he rises and steps back from the throne and to the side.

SYRIAN (*with oily flattery*) We Syrian seers are honoured to
Assist the god-king with our mysteries.
Pharaoh steers the rudders of the sky.
He is sunrise, sunset, east and west;
The sun at noon. The uraeus cobra, on
The royal crown or nemes, with blazing eyes
Shrivels his majesty's enemies.
Pharaoh does not die but walks the Sun's Rays
To the Solar disc. Like great Osiris,
Ruler of the dead, his majesty bears
The emblems of the crook and flail, or wields
The sceptre with the head of Seth the god.
From his girdle hangs the sacred bull's tail
Of the fertile Nile, of Hapi, whom the northerners
Call Apis.

KHYAN (*coldly*) These things all men know. The dreams!

SYRIAN By practising our holy rites of divination,
We've discovered countless meanings of
The royal dreams!

KHYAN (*sternly*) Then you have found nothing!

There are gasps of astonishment as the butler rushes forward and throws himself to the ground before the king.

BUTLER (*in agony*) May the lowliest man in Egypt speak?
May his majesty's butler speak?

KHYAN (*sternly, signalling to him to rise*) He may.

BUTLER *(kneeling)* God pardon me, I *know* of an interpreter
Of dreams! Since first his majesty described
The dreams, my thoughts of guilt have seared me like
Hot metal! To my shame, I lay once in
The royal prison. Two years ago
The god-king pardoned me – restored me
Mercifully to his royal presence.
Before I was released I had a dream,
As did the Memphite baker, my companion. An
Imprisoned Hebrew slave interpreted
Our dreams. Immediately, without a moment's pause,
He prophesied the baker's execution and
My pardon, both in three days' time.

KHYAN Ah yes!
My majesty gave a birthday feast for my
Officials, remembered those in jail,
Condemned or pardoned them.

BUTLER But I forgot
The Hebrew. He is innocent. I promised
I would ask for his release. He was right!
In every detail he was right.

KHYAN My majesty instructs his guards to summon here
The captain of the royal prison for
My majesty to question; also to conduct
The Hebrew – well-attired, clean-shaven – to
This Hall of Audience. My Majesty
Now deigns to listen to the embassy from Tyre.

Exeunt two officials, in haste. Phoenicians emerge from the throng and prostrate themselves before the king, rising as he gives them leave and begins to speak to them privately. Low murmurs of conversation arise here and there in the Hall.

OFFICIAL (*sotto voce*) My young Libyan friend, watch his majesty
Conversing with his face all smiles. They are
Compatriots.

LIBYAN (*in surprise*) The people of Tyre his
Compatriots?

OFFICIAL Certainly. Our king is
The third Phoenician king of Egypt. In
A year when the Egyptian families
Were weak, his People sidled into kingship.There
Was scarcely any bloodshed.

Enter the Captain of the prison, in haste.

LIBYAN Yet he seems
Egyptian to the marrow of his bones.

OFFICIAL (*laughs*) Like a horde of small chameleons climbing the
Papyrus reeds in delta marshland, all
Of them have taken on our colour. – Look
How, with a gracious waft of his royal hand,
His majesty, still smiling, ends their conversation –
(*the Phoenicians step back as the Captain advances towards the throne)* And now – you see the captain of the prison,

Prostrate on the floor before the throne. He's rising,
Speaking eagerly. If only we could hear!

Enter Joseph with two guards.

CAPTAIN . . . In short, this Joseph is a man of absolute
Integrity, a man your majesty can trust.

At a sign from Pharaoh, the Captain steps back. Joseph moves towards the throne, followed by the guards.

LIBYAN (*excitedly*) The captain's standing to one side and an
Egyptian noble is approaching, some proud lord.

OFFICIAL No, it is the Hebrew. Those are prison guards
Escorting him. His majesty has given them
A sign to halt. Now the Hebrew is
The one man moving in this vast and crowded Hall
Of Audience, drawing nearer to the throne. Ssh!

Everyone falls silent

KHYAN So dignified! He travels cloaked in many years
Of grief and bears his head erect above his sorrows!
My majesty enquires: Who is this man?
(*Joseph prostrates himself before the king.*)
Let him rise and speak.

JOSEPH (*calmly*) I am the Hebrew Joseph.

KHYAN Is the Canaanite a prophet? – Are you a prophet?
Like a slim green snake, the Nile twists
And coils across the endless hot red desert,
Flowing, from Elephantine, a hundred

River measures to the Delta mouths
Along the coast. Each year at Elephantine
A surge of mighty waters magically wells
Beneath the river, overfills the Nile bed
And, rushing headlong to the sea, bursts all
The banks of the stupendous god. Shouldering
His way across the barren land, the Nile
Thrusts east and west to reach the limit of
His impetus, long weeks remains a giant lake,
Then inch by inch subsides, retreats within
His former bounds, leaving in his wake
A valley floor of fertile mud. Each year
The Nile Inundation makes this land
The granary of many races who
Surround the Great Green sea; while in the
Nile marshlands livestock finds rich grazing.
My majesty has had two dreams – of grain,
Of cattle – ominous dreams. I fear for Egypt.

JOSEPH Will his majesty describe the dreams?

KHYAN Standing by the Nile, I watched the flow
Of empty water. I saw no herdsmen,
Paddling boats of bundled reeds, or wading
Warily; but seven head of cattle
Rose up in the foreground, wading from
The river on to land – sleek handsome beasts.
I blinked and saw the seven of them grazing
In a meadow. Then seven haggard
Cattle clambered from the Nile with searching
Hooves. Over starkly jutting bones their skin
Was taut. They swallowed up the grazing beasts
But still looked starved. The interpretation?

JOSEPH May I hear the second dream?

KHYAN On a stalk
I saw seven ears of corn grow ripe and full.
Another seven, thin and shrivelled, scorched
To nothing by the east wind's blast, then sprang
Up from the ground and swallowed up the first.
The interpretation?

JOSEPH Both dreams are one. The Nile Inundation
Will give us seven years of plenty – well-fed beasts,
Good harvests. Then come seven lean years which
Will swallow our abundance, and we'll starve.
For seven years the Nile flood will be too low.

KHYAN Ah! So simple! Undoubtedly right.
A terrible warning!

JOSEPH There will be famine in the land unless . . .

KHYAN Unless?

JOSEPH Let Egypt find a man discreet and wise,
An organiser, a dynamic man
Like Imhotep; like Imhotep, the vizier
Of great king Zoser, in whose reign, a thousand years
Ago, a similar calamity occurred:
Seven fertile floods preceded seven
Years of want. Let the State claim in
Taxation, not a tenth of Egypt's produce, as
Is customary, but one fifth. The fifth
Of barley and of emmer should be stored
To be our food supply in coming years

Of harvest failure. Grain kept dry, well-stored,
Will keep indefinitely, staying palatable and
Remaining always equally nutritious.

KHYAN (*triumphantly*) Aha! A natural administrator. –
Speak on! Continue!

JOSEPH In the years when food
Is scarce, let the population pay the State
For grain with money, personal possessions,
Then with livestock, lastly ceding to
The king their title to the land. As always, great
Estates belonging to the Temples will
Control the distribution of their own supplies.

KHYAN My majesty is almost speechless with
Astonishment. In you the gods have wrought
A statesman for our years of need, a saviour
Sculpted from the rock of suffering.
I hear God's spirit speak in every word!
(*commandingly*) My Lords, our trusted vizier is dying –
Choose this man as his successor!
Can any doubt that Joseph, dredged up in
This hour from the depths of life, should be
The vizier of our Lands? The king demands
Advice from Nekhebu, his councillor.

NEKHEBU (*fervently*) The Hebrew is the providential man,
The *man* of the hour, of the day,
Exalted now by Egypt's wisest king!

KHYAN (*swiftly*) It is not the habit of my majesty
To act in haste, but here immortal hands

Point out the way of safety through the Evil time.
Joseph is vizier. Grace will come to us through *him*.
Does the council of my majesty approve?

COUNCILLORS We approve his majesty's decision!

KHYAN Good! There is no contrary opinion!
My majesty asks Joseph: Is he ready to
Accept the vizier's office?

JOSEPH (*firmly*) I accept. *(he kneels)*

KHYAN We will proceed to the investiture.
Zaphnath-Paneah is Joseph's new, Egyptian name.
With *this* gold ring, which bears the royal seal,
My majesty confers on him authority
To rule the nation. Vizier, wear it. Let
The jewelled necklace of a nobleman
Be clasped around our vizier's neck. No man
Has greater wisdom than our vizier;
The gods have made this plain. Rise, vizier!

Two officials leave in haste at a signal from Khyan.

OFFICIAL (*to Libyan*) Look at him, my friend. An hour ago
He was in jail, deprived of hope. Today
This man has soared more swiftly than the sun
To Egypt's zenith. His expression has
Not changed! What admirable gravitas!

The two officials reenter with a necklace, a gold chain of office and a papyrus scroll. In obedience to Nekhebu's gestures Joseph kneels momentarily as Nekhebu fastens the necklace for him.

NEKHEBU (*loudly*) The vizier's as unfathomable as
The immortal gods who, golden-faced,.
With plaited beards like lapis-lazuli,
Dwell beside the Elysian lake of lilies.

Joseph kneels before Khyan as Nekhebu takes from the second official the chain of office and, bowing low, offers it to the king, taking care not to touch him.

KHYAN Vizier, bow your head. Receive from royal hands
Your chain of office. See the golden pendant,
Tiny seated statue, with the ostrich
Feather poised above her head, of Ma'at,
Ra's daughter, who is Truth and Justice.
Wear her always to remind you of
The need for virtue in your judgments. Rise!

NEKHEBU Favour neither rich nor poor. In the
Notorious case: The Eloquent Peasant And
The Donkey Trespasser, the peasant's rich
Accuser was a perjurer. The law was weak;
Only the peasant's own tenacity saved
The face of Justice. In the Case Of The
Unjust Vizier, Kheti was the vizier who,
Afraid of being thought unjust, found
Against his relatives' just cause. All
Injustice is abhorrent to the gods.

KHYAN The vizier is a prince in Egypt.
His justice is impartial. The vizier shall
Be wrathful only where immortal fury would
Be justified. Fear of Egypt's vizier is
A great deterrent, for the River Nile
And its breezes carry word of all

His judgments into every home. Zaphnath–
Paneah, *this* must be your stature.

NEKHEBU The vizier's the support and strength
Of every life, the Shelter of the weak.
He shields the helpless from the haughty.

KHYAN The vizier is Egypt's Judge and Egypt's Chief
Administrator; under his control
Are Irrigation, Agriculture, Transport, Trade
And Building; Law, the Treasury, the Royal Estates.

NEKHEBU The vizier is our Defence, protector of
Our Lands of the Papyrus and the Lotus,
Protector of the king. He is copper round
The gold of Egypt's throne. His is a bitter task.

Nekhebu again beckons to the servant who this time presents him with the scroll, which Nekhebu hands to the king, as carefully as before.

KHYAN Zaphnath-Paneah, read from this papyrus scroll
The final oath.

Joseph receives the scroll from the hands of the king.

JOSEPH I swear that I shall strive,
Unceasingly, to make my every action as
Your vizier acceptable to God; to be
The impartial judge and just administrator of
The nation.

KHYAN (*warmly*) You are blest, dear friend. Through you,
Our Egypt will be blest. I now confer
On you the title: 'Sole Companion of

The King'. Few members of my court are granted it.
A guard of honour shall precede you everywhere
You go. Tomorrow, yours shall be the second
Royal Chariot in the lion hunt.
Lord Councillors, my Council in the Hall
Of Audience is at an end. The path
Of our new vizier now lies clear before
Him. Only one more question needs to be
Decided; that of charm and grace and beauty.
Whom shall he marry? Come, Zaphnath-Paneah,
Let me lean upon your shoulder as I
Leave the hall. I will give the matter of
Your marriage careful thought.

There is a trumpet fanfare as Pharaoh rises from the throne.

USHERS (*strike the floor once*) Tremble, the god is coming!
(*strike the floor once*) Tremble, the god is coming!
(*strike the floor once*) Tremble, the god is coming!

(*Exeunt Joseph and Khyan.)*

SCENE III

A room in the house of Asenath's father in Avaris. Enter Asenath and Tuya.

ASENATH (*romantically*) Zaphnath-Paneah is the vizier's
Official name, but 1 shall call him Joseph in
The privacy of home. I'm longing for
Our wedding day!

TUYA (*briskly*) That's fortunate. At first you thought
Him alien and wished that he would go away.

ASENATH (*laughs*) Yes, but when Potiphera, my father, brought
The amazing news, I was beside myself with joy.
'Dear Asenath!' he said. 'Such an honour!
Khyan has arranged your marriage to
The vizier of Egypt!' I thought I'd passed
Unnoticed. How thrilled I was! Soon I would
Be married and my husband had been chosen by
The king himself!

TUYA Small wonder! Your actions are
Like incense in the air, my pet. Your goodness is
A glowing lamp in all our lives.

ASENATH (*warmly*) You've always been
So generous! – My life has been transformed.
You'll understand how much I yearned to worship
Egypt's vizier – at first sight.

TUYA (*her voice suggests she is suppressing a smile*)
Naturally.

ASENATH In feverish excitement in the jewelled, painted hall,
I scanned the white-clad company,
Was shown the vizier, standing with
His back to me. Eagerly I watched.
He turned. I saw his face. I saw a man
Whom I would not have chosen. Speaking to him I
Was timid, overawed.

TUYA You will have charmed him!

ASENATH (*modestly*) He has said I did. And when my father
Questioned me, I hid my disappointment.
Later I was glad I had concealed
My shameful blindness. To have encountered such
A man, without at once perceiving who
He was! At last I saw, and murmured:
'This man's soul, thank heaven, transcends mine'.

TUYA So it does, it does. or rather, he is like
Yourself, but infinitely stronger – as he needs
To be. He carries Egypt on his shoulders.

JOSEPH (*off*) Is the Lady Asenath at home?

ASENATH (*nervously*) Whose voice is that? It is the vizier's.
Isis, Mother of God, Lady of Heaven!

TUYA I'll leave you, Lady Asenath.

Enter Servant.

SERVANT The lord vizier!

Exeunt Servant and Tuya. Enter Joseph.

JOSEPH Asenath!

ASENATH My Joseph. (*They embrace.*)

JOSEPH (*softly*) You are fresh water in the desert. Why
Do you turn your head?

ASENATH (*quietly, simply*) I am overcome.

JOSEPH You do not know your power. I see you, and
The clamour of the world dies like an echo.
I am at peace.

ASENATH Peace is not your gift to me.
Your soul surrounds me like a burning fire.
In the fire's heart I cannot breathe!

JOSEPH I have stood on Gerizim, looked down
Upon a sea of cloud; quiet drifts,
Eternal stillness. That is your serenity.

ASENATH How different it is for me! I am
A tiny creature, held in your vast,
Transfiguring love, held in a massive hand.
My love, you are not maimed and warped like other men;
You are whole.

JOSEPH That is an illusion, Asenath.
If I seem whole, it is because of you.
At last I can accept my exile. Your love soothes
My yearning for my long lost family, (*the hint of a laugh*)
Making it endurable, my love;
Yes, Asenath, your magic heals the heart that bled.
(*calmly*) This is what I dreamed the power of love might be.

ASENATH (*simply*) Surely the purpose of the world, of all
Mortality, is love. Love should be
The only theme of human ingenuity.
We're placed on earth to find a million million ways
Of saying: 'I love.'

JOSEPH You are right. I see
It daily in the courts. Dishonest men
Have lost the centre of their being. Come,
My sweet, we'll stroll awhile beside the Nile,
And watch flamingoes feed in the shallows.

SCENE IV

The Court of Justice in Avaris, with a Judge in a robe of white linen seated on a chair, Constables, Officials, the prisoners Abana and Ribaddi on stools between Prison Guards and a scribe sitting cross-legged on the ground with ink-pallet and papyrus scroll before him on a low table.

OFFICIAL The lord vizier!

Enter Joseph.

JOSEPH (*sternly*) The Avaris Justice Court is now in session.
My lord judge, you received my message?

JUDGE I did, lord vizier. These two men here
Were sentenced yesterday; their punishment
Includes imprisonment.

JOSEPH (*with authority*) Good. My lord,
I will address the court. I will remind
And warn all here: Do not swear by Pharaoh!
If you invoke the king and are a liar,
Dark powers threaten him. The king
Is Truth and Justice. Falsehood injures him.

Lies are darkness that devours the light.
Priestly magic ritual will save
The king from evil, but the perjured man
Is *dead*, who swore by Pharaoh.
It is the law. I must enforce it. –
Let no man, innocent or guilty, swear
By Pharaoh! Scribe, you have recorded all
My words. Let them be the preamble
To every session of the courts throughout
The land. Let them be spoken loudly.
Lives will be saved.

JUDGE Take warning from the sage
Advice of our lord vizier. Constable, describe,
Please, yesterday's two cases showing people
Who put things where they did not belong.

CONSTABLE (*clears throat importantly and speaks with relish*)
Milords – lord vizier, and officials of
The court, this man here, Abana, is a farmer.
In the annual flood he moved his boundary stones
To include a large slice of his neighbour's land.
We proved the truth of this from land-surveyors'
Records for the previous tax assessment.
Whereupon the accused declared the Nile flood
Had moved the stones, but the erect, deeply
imbedded
Posture of the stones was further proof – *he lied.*

JUDGE Lord vizier, five times the land Abana tried
To steal has been awarded from his own
Land to his injured neighbour. Also Abana has
Been sent to jail.

CONSTABLE This other wealthy farmer,
Called Ribaddi, yes, Ribaddi, accused a man
Of carrying *off* his treasured piebald goat. True,
His goat was grazing in his neighbour's herd,
But Ribaddi was seen by witnesses,
Two men who did not know each other.
Depositing his piebald goat *within*
His guiltless neighbour's herd. Case – dismissed!

JUDGE Ribaddi, found guilty yesterday, must pay
His neighbour with a herd of goats – and serve
A prison sentence.

JOSEPH (*coldly*) Here in Egypt all
Our agricultural labourers must give Corvée –
That is, their labour to the State – for one
Flood season out of every four. This is now
The vizier's decree: Criminals may not
Lie idle in our prisons, but must dig
And build for Egypt all year long. Your first
Offender – two years' toil: Your second, four –
Two years more for casting guilt upon
The innocent. Let the vizier's decrees,
Made known today, be promulgated everywhere
In Egypt.

SCRIBE My lord, it shall be done.

SCENE V

A garden in the palace of Avaris. Birds are singing. Enter Khyan and Nekhebu.

KHYAN You tell me, Nekhebu, that our new vizier
Embodies the Egyptian ideal?

NEKHEBU (*enthusiastically*) Your majesty, on his behalf *already* I
Could write his Epitaph!

KHYAN How would it run?

NEKHEBU Like our noblest ancestors our vizier
Already merits these words carved in diorite:
'I've given to widows and to orphans and
Protected them. To every man that worked
For me I've paid good wages. If a man
Was hungry, I fed him. If he was thirsty,
I gave him to drink. If he was naked,
I clothed him; if lacking oil to soothe his limbs,
I gave him oil; if lacking *deben* for
His fare across the Nile, I paid the ferryman
Or let my servant row him to the other bank.'

KHYAN (*delightedly*) Yes, yes, all this is true of
Zathnath-Paneah.
Remind me – Where is our rendezvous this
morning?

NEKHEBU The sites of two large granaries where you
Will lay foundation stones and bury sets

Of ceremonial tools. That is where
The vizier is at work today. Since we're
Expecting higher floods, new granaries
Will be erected further from the Nile,
In dry red desert. Curving courses for
The brickwork will ensure that seeping water in
The ground below will cause no cracks. Our granaries
Will sail like ships upon the waters of the flood.

KHYAN (*with vivacity*) Par excellence an Organiser!
Everywhere
A man of vigour and good sense! In the courts
These are his punishments – generally
Repayment plus hard labour – that's for theft,
Etcetera; prison for the violent; death
For indescribable atrocity.
I admire his mercy – and the terrifying mask
He wears in court which overawes
Our criminals, inspiring superstitious dread.
Lately, two confessed in court to robberies
Of which they weren't accused. Our vizier's a man
Of serpentine and charitable wisdom!

NEKHEBU And may I ask: What of the family who had
Him jailed, on false testimony, in
Your predecessor's reign?

KHYAN Ah! Dimly I
Remember hearing what became of them.
Zaphnath-Paneah is not vindictive. No.
'Their story is for me,' he said, 'a flight of steps
That ends in a blank wall. The matter is forgotten.'

NEKHEBU *(nodding to himself)* He is exemplary, in every way.

KHYAN He is also happy, happy with his wife.
It was a natural choice, to offer him
A high priest's young and gentle daughter.
He is a happy man at last.
Come, Nekhebu, let us go to meet him.

Exeunt Khyan and Nekhebu.

SCENE VI

A bedroom in the house of Joseph and Asenath in Avaris with one single bed.

ASENATH We have been married one short month.

JOSEPH A month
Of bliss and sweetness, honey and water lilies.
I'd endure my life in prison for a second time
To marry you.

ASENATH (*murmurs*) And being thrown into the well?

JOSEPH That made me shed a Nile of tears. 'How could
They?' is the saddest of all human questions,
Asked by men who' re victims of Man's hate,
Their brothers' Hate. And *why* hate? Who would grip
A sharpened blade without a haft?
Yet men hold on to hate and let it lacerate
Their lives – their own first victim and their worst.
I know because I hated Judah, till
I saw my hate was – love turned inside out,

Love desperately hamm'ring at the gates
Of men who'd never answer, a plea for love.
I ceased to be at war with me, but life
Became long yearning for my father – and
He may have died – and, for my brothers,
Most of all for Benjamin who, if he
Is alive, believes me dead.

ASENATH When you were a youth you dreamed of all
Your brothers, Reuben, Judah, *all* of them,
With Leah and your father Jacob, bowing
To the ground before you. Now you're lord of
Egypt, second only to his majesty.
And they will *come*. They are coming, and will
Kne-el, paying homage, begging your forgiveness.

JOSEPH *(with the ghost of a laugh)* Don't say that, Asenath!
You must not teach me to expect them daily.
How many hours have I waited?
I may need to wait as many hours and years
Again, before God sends my brothers south.
My obsession must remain a patient one. –
Sweet life, you'll never understand your powers
Of consolation. After years of violent storms,
You offer peace.

ASENATH (*simply*) How beautiful is Egypt and her gods,
A land of dignity and spiritual peace,
Basking in sun, glinting with merriment.
How beautiful is married love. I am like
The bennu bird, the sacred heron of Osiris.
At the rising of the sun, while ostriches
In wadis dance for joy, I fly above the river
In the burning rays: Fire over water

In the morning sun. I am the phoenix
Burned to ashes in the sunburst; reborn again
To soar across the enamel sky unscathed.
Weary, I alight upon the willow tree,
And fold my wings.

JOSEPH Everything is sacrosanct.

ASENATH My love, you are my only love.

JOSEPH Go to sleep in my spirit, queen of light.
You are cherished in me till the end of time.
I know your soul. Nothing can take it from me.
Love is not as strong as death, but stronger.
I will love you all the days of my life
And all the days of my death. Your soul in mine,
One single unity, shall never be
Two selves again. You know already your
Eternal life and my eternal company.
I keep you safe, fortress spirit round
Frail Asenath. Were I dead, Asenath
Would find me living with her still . . .

ASENATH Our two merged spirits clasping with my hand
The lion-headed armrests of the chair;
Raising the roller blind to enter through
The doorway, setting the folding stool within
The kiosk in the garden; making green
Baboons pick fig-tree fruit, plucking long–
Stemmed lotus lilies from the formal pond,
Struggling with both hands and writhing back,
To pull above my head the tubular
White linen dress, pouring water from
The *zir*, drawing back the sheet upon

The narrow bed and touching the head-rest
Of the resurrection.

JOSEPH
So I in death
Would live in Asenath. As for the destiny
Of living on together, O my queen,
Rejoice! You are the passion of my life,
The absolute; none comparable before;
No sensual-spiritual love can follow.
Give yourself up to me in boundless trust.
Nothing can be wrong between you and me.
Trust the man who kneels with his head in the dust
Before Almighty God, receives his strength
From God, and rises up to serve, to serve
On every side, and keep you in his strength.
Neither to God nor you will he be guilty of
Apostasy. I offer shelter for
Your threefold beauty, Asenath; beauty
Of soul and mind and body, such as I
Have always sought; need also, such as I
Have always sought. I shall call you Nanufar,
'The Beautiful'. Ah, my love!

ACT III

THE SPHINX

SCENE I

A granary at Avaris. Several men are leaving the site, each one carrying a full sack.Donkeys can be heard braying offstage.A line of bales of hay partially dividing the stage in two suggests the language barrier between Hebrew and Egyptian.

PEASANT Sir, I am grateful for this sack of grain.

OVERSEER (*jocosely*) *Now* you peasants *see* why you were
doubly taxed –
And why for *seven* years tax officials claimed
Two tithes of grain in tax and stored it in
State Granaries like this! – There's wisdom in it, for
By rights, last year or this, you should have starved
To death. Today you stand here, thanks to our
Great Egypt's vizier, *breathing,* privileged
To eat, and able to buy all your food
At ordinary prices. – No question of
Extortion, you'll agree.

PEASANT No, sir. Thank you, sir.

Exit peasant as eight of Joseph's brothers enter joyfully, Judah leading the way, Simeon and Levi following him; then Dan with Naphtali and Gad; Asher, then Issachar. Donkeys bray off-stage.

JUDAH My brothers, here's the grain-store – our great hope
For saving all our families in Hebron from
Starvation. Jacob was right to send us down
To Egypt. On our journey we've met strings
Of donkeys laden with Egyptian corn.
Large silos here – no sign of shortage. Promising!

OVERSEER (*aside*) Ageing, bearded Canaanites the vizier wants
To see. I think we have some here. (*loudly* You there!
Where are you from?

JUDAH You are the overseer?
We've come from Hebron in the land of Canaan.

OVERSEER I've heard about you Canaanites. Drought! The Nile
In the Sky of Canaan shed no rain this year.
The Nile itself has failed – low floods, poor crops,
But we have shown un-*u*-sual foresight.
(*Shouts on several different notes*)
Assistant Granary Overseer, where are you?

Enter Assistant.

OVERSEER Ah, there you are! (*in a stage whisper*) Run to fetch my lord
The vizier as fast as legs will take you. Tell him:
'Bearded Canaanites from Hebron, middle-aged.'

Exit Assistant.

OVERSEER (*aside*) I will observe them closely. Perhaps
They're guilty men whom our lord vizier must judge.
He takes a look at all the older men from Canaan.

JUDAH Here's somewhere sensible *at last* in this
Benighted land – the first place free of women!

LEVI Judah, you are right. The market place
Was swarming with young females – hardly a man
In sight. A shopkeeper I questioned said:
'The men are in their houses, weaving.'

JUDAH (*utters a laugh*) Certain that
You'd swallow it. He said it in the fixed belief
All foreigners are simpletons.

LEVI It could be true.
The women go unveiled. The servant class
Are practically unclothed. All glance at you
With interest as they pass. (*amused*) And here comes Reuben.

Enter Reuben.

JUDAH (*laughing*) Reuben, you look bruised and – disillusioned.

REUBEN (*out of breath*) The city of my dreams, I thought this was.
What a fool! I offered money to
A bold-faced woman, only to receive
A drubbing from her servants, whom I hadn't spied
Among the crowd. 'Didn't I offer her
Enough?' I asked them when they paused for breath.

'I noticed she was wearing sandals. Is
She in a higher income bracket?'
After another beating it emerged
She was the wife of a High Priest of such
And such a god, First Prophet, Digger of
Canals – in short the woman of a family
Illustrious in Egypt. How was I to know?

Enter Zebulun.

And here is Zebulun, look, look – still starry-eyed!

ZEBULUN (*with zest*) I note from all our tethered donkeys that I'm last.
Have you bought grain already? I have seen marvels!
Gold is as common here as wayside dust,
They say, and I can quite believe it. Palaces
And temples built for men as tall as palm trees!
I never could have dreamt of such magnificence.

JUDAH All present and correct, my brothers! Time
To approach the granary official.

VOICES (*off*) The vizier! The vizier! Stand back!

Enter Joseph, Interpreter and Guards.

JOSEPH (*aside*) These men in greying middle age must be
The travellers from Hebron.(*electrified*) Great heavens!
I think they *are* my brothers. After twenty years!
My senses reel. Can that be Judah? Is it Reuben
There beside him? My brothers, have you come at last?

(*in anguish*) The shock is like a mortal blow.
Benjamin!
Which one is Benjamin? Can Benjamin
Be dead? And where is Jacob? – God of Israel, I
Need iron strength. Will they know me? (*loudly*)
Interpreter,
I'll speak through you.

INTERPRETER Hebrews, the vizier
Himself will answer your Petition.

JOSEPH Hebrews! You see in me the vizier,
Lord of Egypt, Pharaoh's Lord Chief Justice,
First man in all the land below Great Egypt's king.

Interpreter begins translating to group of brothers.

JOSEPH (*in an undertone*) I see here all the sons of Leah,
the sons
Of Bilhah and the sons of Zilpah, but –
But not my Benjamin. Is he alive? (*utters a groan*)
My road is never easy. Benjamin!

JUDAH Lord vizier, we, the humble servants of
The lord of Egypt, offer silver for
Egyptian corn, to save our starving families
In Hebron. We beg you: Favour our request!

Interpreter begins translating to Joseph.

JUDAH (*aghast*) My brothers, note the vizier's threatening
face.
Bow down to the ground again.

JOSEPH *(harshly)* Interpreter,
Say now: It would be better for these men
If they confessed the truth. I know them for
An army sent by Egypt's enemies.

Interpreter translates to brothers.

JOSEPH *(aside, urgently)* Where are my younger brother and my father Jacob?
(after a deep breath) I must not weaken. Even after years
Of practice, I am barely strong enough for this.
(with yearning) My brothers, here at last, so close to me!

JUDAH *(in desperation)* Assure my lord the vizier we are not
An army! All of us are brothers, one man's sons.
We've travelled here from Hebron in the land of Canaan.

Interpreter translates to Joseph.

JOSEPH *(aside, in tears)* *Control*, impatient heart! I must not show
My overwhelming feelings for my kin,
My flesh and blood. I must not falter. *(to brothers, harshly)*
Ten of you, and all from Canaan? I say
You are spies, here to reconnoitre our
Defences for a *foreign* power and
Its hostile armies. You shall not live
To tell your tale to Egypt's enemies!

Interpreter translates to brothers.

JOSEPH (*aside*) How sadly changed they are by age, all seamed
And wrinkled, faces creased like much-worn garments.
That is how their eyes see Egypt's vizier – oldish,
Battered by experience, marked by time –
And by no stretch of the imagination
Can this foreign prince be long lost Joseph.

JUDAH (*utters a cry of despair*) No, no, I must protest! We are innocent!
Without Egyptian grain our families
Will die of hunger! We are honest men, not spies!

Interpreter translates to Joseph.

JUDAH (*in an undertone*) My brothers, bow down yet again.
We must placate this terrifying nobleman.
He is listening balefully to the interpreter.
He holds our families' survival in his hand.
Suddenly I fear for all their lives.

JOSEPH (*harshly*) *I* say – these men are lying in their teeth!
Tell them the vizier knows exactly who they are.
He *knows* their purpose is reconnaissance
Before an enemy assault! Espionage!
(*coldly*) In Egypt spies are put to death, for treachery.

Interpreter translates to brothers.

JOSEPH (*aside*) Jacob, Benjamin, where are you? (*through tears*) Surely,
Surely they'll come out with what I need to know!

REUBEN Lord vizier, your suspicions are without foundation!

LEVI (*eagerly*) Reuben, yes, convince him we are harmless!

REUBEN Lord of Egypt, we are your humblest servants.
We are brothers, twelve in all. The youngest's with
Our father at this time. Our father sent us.

Interpreter translates to Joseph.

JOSEPH (*aside, as the interpreter speaks*) At last! They are alive!
Benjamin and my father are alive! (*a sob*)
I'll need to hide my tears of gratitude.

REUBEN As for the twelfth, long ago he disappeared.

Brief murmur from Interpreter to Joseph.

JUDAH Reuben, Simeon, I am filled with dread.
The air we breathe is charged with menace.
The Lord of Egypt either turns his back,
Or glares implacably.

JOSEPH (*wrathfully*) By all the gods, you Hebrews try my patience!
Madness, to think of trying to deceive me!

Interpreter begins to translate to brothers.

JUDAH (*loudly*) My brothers, kneel down in the dust, before
The stern and mighty man of Egypt.

JOSEPH (*aside*) Suddenly the dream I dreamed in youth becomes
A scene in life. The smoke of prophecy
Takes living form. Is it possible not *one*
Of all these brothers can interpret what
Is happening? One at least should see and should
Cry out: 'This is the dream! The vizier
Is Joseph!' I, who am inspiring fear,
Tremble with awe before the occult power.
Ah! Reuben is about to speak.

REUBEN (*steadily*) O mighty prince,
Our father sent us for our children's sake.
Lord vizier, believe us! 'Why wait for food
To drop from heaven? Egypt has grain to sell.
There's corn in Egypt. Buy food there!' he said.

Interpreter translates briefly to Joseph.

JOSEPH (*sternly*) Prove it! And till it's proved you'll all stay here
In prison, all but one – and he must travel home
To Canaan – *if* that is your place of origin –
And bring the youngest brother who, you claim, exists
To see me here in Egypt. Failing confirmation
From this brother – by the Life of Pharaoh
You'll be executed! Guards, conduct these rogues to jail!
Guard them with your lives! Ten brothers? Never!

Interpreter translates to brothers.

JOSEPH (*aside, firmly*) Their minds will spin a web of terror as
They lie in prison. What shape? – We shall see. – That was

The worst. I've overcome my overpowering urge
To weep on Judah's breast. Resigned to patience, I
Am following the proper path. I can be patient
For another year if need be. (*with sudden emotion*)
I must wait!

JUDAH (*kneels*) Must we rot in prison as our children starve?
We beg the vizier for mercy! Spare us!

JOSEPH Silence! – Guards! Take away the spies!

SCENE II

The same. Joseph and Interpreter (both concealed) and Overseer watch the arrival of Joseph's brothers under guard.

OVERSEER (*aside*) The Canaanites have spent three days in jail
And are returning under escort to
The granary. 'Overseer, be ready,' said
The vizier's messenger. Today these aliens
Look shifty-eyed and guilty – except for
One man who is like – a thunderstorm.

JOSEPH They're all
Assembled. So . . . interpreter, step forward. I
Shall start by being a hidden listener.

Interpreter emerges.

JUDAH Patience, Simeon!

SIMEON (*scornfully*) Three days in jail because
The Egyptian vizier is afraid of shadows.
I despise him!

JUDAH (*sternly*) Simeon, quiet! Conceal your anger!

SIMEON Is all of Israel cowed, because a bureaucrat
Has spoken harshly? (*sneeringly*) Am I the only *man*
In Israel's tribe? Can these trembling fools
Be Simeon's brothers?

JUDAH (*in bitter but controlled grief*) Simeon, we are cowed
By all the images that rise up in
Our tarnished conscience and condemn us.
The difference between ourselves and you
This day, is not that we've no courage, but
That you've no conscience – or, if you have one,
It is stifled in the rubble of
Your unrepented sins. In these three days
The rest of us have found out we are guilty;
Guilty, to all intents, of fratricide.
I accuse – myself!

JOSEPH (*aside, after a groan*) Noble Judah!

ZEBULUN (*stirringly*) I, Zebulun, accuse myself. Our helpless
Brother begged for mercy while a ring
Of devils stood about him, laughing. Answering tears
With cruelty is the lowest human crime –
Gloating sadism to a weeping brother. –
All this is happening to us because of what
We did to Joseph.This is what we earned that year.
We owe our grief. We owe our terror and
Our death. We reap the harvest we have sown.

If the vizier knew what we had done,
He'd kill us, not for Egypt's sake, but
To avenge the human race.

JOSEPH *(aside, through his tears)* Such remorse,
My brother Zebulun? Moving, moving.

LEVI (*sternly*) I, Levi, now accept the penalty of death
As just.

SIMEON (*furiously*) If we've been brought from prison now
To face our execution – nine snivelling
Lunatics will die with one brave man!

REUBEN I told you all we shouldn't harm the boy.

JUDAH (*sharply*) When it counted, Reuben, you weren't there
To throw your weight into the balance.

REUBEN Earlier
I'd stopped you all from stabbing him.

JUDAH (*appeasingly*) Reuben,
It's myself I'm angry with, not you.

REUBEN (*sadly*) More than Joseph could, I blame myself.

JOSEPH (*aside*) You are right, my faithful Reuben. Time for me to appear.

Joseph emerges frowning and, except for Simeon, all his brothers fall to their knees.

A GUARD (*in alarm*) The vizier! My lord the vizier,
Zaphnath-Paneah!

JOSEPH (*commandingly*) First, interpreter,
You are to tell the Hebrews they may rise.
Tell them also, if they do exactly as
I say, not one of them shall lose his life.

Interpreter translates to brothers.

JUDAH (*sighs with relief*) My brothers, we've been granted a reprieve.

JOSEPH (*briskly*) Interpreter, say this: 'Because I fear God
You shall have a chance to save yourselves. One
Among you is to stay in prison here.
I will suppose your story true and give
You grain to feed your households. Bring to me
Your youngest brother when you next need food
And, by so doing, prove you've told the truth.
But – come without him and I'll know you lied.
Then by the Life of Pharaoh you are spies
Who still shall pay with blood!'

Interpreter translates to brothers.

JOSEPH (*aside, kindly*) What progress you have made in jail, my brothers!
You have disinterred your most unnatural crime,
Long-buried, long-forgotten – and repent
With great intensity. Identifying with
Your victim's misery, you see yourselves
As bullies without mercy. Only Simeon
Remains as hard as bronze, ignorant of
The workings of his soul, of his deformity.

JUDAH Which brother will the vizier pick? He'll live
In fear of death, till we bring Benjamin.

LEVI

Reduced from nine deaths to a lottery
For one. Any moment now the vizier
Will choose his hostage.

JUDAH

(*sadly*) Still my heart is weighed
Down with my horror, with my dread, as I
Relive my cruelty to Joseph. Though the vizier
May intend us mercy, there's no mercy in
The memory of long-past guilt, no way to lift
The burden of that knowledge from my soul.
And we are still in trouble, brothers, trouble that
Has surely overtaken us because of Joseph –
Retribution, justice. All of this is just.
Remember Joseph crying out he loved us?
Remember how we preyed on him like carrion crows
Savaging him, throwing him in the well,
Mocking at him as we sold him? Sold Him! (*a sob*) God forgive me! I should be the one
To stay in Egypt! – Poor boy, poor boy!
How could I do it? He stood there dirty,
Swollen-eyed, tears streaming down his face.

REUBEN

The vizier's standing with his back to us again.

JOSEPH

(*aside, with controlled grief*) If a man repents in tears of what
He finds he's done, that man is good.

ZEBULUN

We feel
As you do, Judah – look about you! Dan has wild
Eyes raised to heaven, Asher's clutching at
His head. Bodies, faces, all express
Despair, until we come to Simeon,

With folded arms, who glares ferociously
At everyone in sight.

REUBEN (*sadly*) O Judah, I should be
The one to stay in Egypt. – I loved Joseph and
I sought him out, because I knew that he
Was better than myself. Often it fell to me
To save him from the anger of the rest
Of you. Exasperation I could feel,
But never, never, envious hatred.
That fatal day I was the only man
With normal sight among the blinded and
Bedevilled. The blood guilt is on all our heads,
Because I stayed too long with women. (*a groan*)

JUDAH (*in an undertone*) The vizier's back is turned again. Thank heaven
He knows no Hebrew! He has whirled round, frowning.

JOSEPH (*with authority*) Guards, take the man I touch and bind his arms
With leather thongs. Fetter his feet with copper chains.
(*to interpreter*) Inform the Hebrews, *this* man is the one
I say shall live in an Egyptian jail until
They come again to Egypt with their youngest brother.

Interpreter speaks briefly, eliciting a roar of rage from Simeon.

JUDAH (*excitedly, in an undertone*) Simeon! He's chosen Simeon!

SIMEON (*in a frenzy*) Take your hands off me! (*He fights the guards, panting and roaring with fury*) Hell and damnation!
Let me go! Damn you all!

JOSEPH Guards! On entering
The prison, see that man is soundly thrashed.
Contempt for Egypt's justice must be punished.
Interpreter, accompany the Hebrews and
Interpret for them as they buy their food.
Overseer, a word with you.

Exeunt Simeon and guards.

OVERSEER Yes, my lord.

JOSEPH (*in an undertone*) Overseer, when your men have filled
The Hebrews' sacks, replace the Hebrews' silver in
The neck of each man's sack. Fill their
Donkeys' panniers with food for men and
Provender for beasts – enough to take them back
To Canaan. Act without the Hebrews' knowledge.

OVERSEER My lord, your word is law.

Exit Joseph.

SCENE III

The courtyard of an inn on a route leading to the Egyptian border at Silḙ. Donkeys bray offstage. Enter Judah, Levi, Zebulun and Reuben.

JUDAH (*soberly*) All the same, we'll stay to eat the meal
They're making ready at this inn. Steady, steady.
Let's all try to keep our heads; not hare
Off screeching like a panic-stricken army. Well!
The problem's this, my brothers: While unloading, in
The neck of every sack of corn we found
A pouch containing all the silver that we'd paid
The granary. Therefore – we've paid nothing for
Our food and look like thieves. – Worse still, our animals
Are laden with supplies we never thought
To ask for. Thus – it looks as though we've helped
Ourselves in Egypt with a liberal hand.

LEVI (*swiftly*) It's a pretext for the vizier to jail
Us all again – today, tomorrow, who knows when.
I am afraid.

ZEBULUN Couldn't it be accidental?

JUDAH No. It was deliberate – but why? (*laughs*) Perhaps
It's an apology for our incarceration.
Consider, brothers. To the man who knows
That he is guilty, even kindness and
Benevolence can seem a threat.

REUBEN The vizier

Is harsh. Would his right hand whip us while his left
Hand showered us with blessings?

ZEBULUN Visualise
The hardships of our journey home – without
All these mysterious gifts. A guardian angel
Is protecting us.

JUDAH (*humorously*) Good, Zebulun. Then if
We are accused, we will explain: ‘It was an angel’.

LEVI (*grimly*) I have a presentiment of evil.
I seem to hear Great Egypt’s warriors
Thund’ring after us in chariots.

REUBEN No, Levi – for the small fry such as us,
They’d use their hunter runners with their tracker dogs.
Naturally with the same result. I wish
We could be free of this uneasiness.
No, call it by it’s name. It’s fear.

JUDAH We are unnerved. (*decisively*)
We’ll eat, and make what time we can. The mighty hand
Of Egypt’s spread above us, shadowing our journey.

SCENE IV

Jacob's Camp in Hebron with Jacob sitting in the shade of an awning. Judah, Reuben and Levi sit nearby. Dinah stands before her father.

DINAH (*hounding him*) But Jacob, soon there will be no more grain.
Then how shall all the women of the tribe
Make shift to feed you?

JACOB You keep prodding me
And goading me as if I were an ox.
I can't send Benjamin away to Egypt.

DINAH Am I to let the children starve without
A murmur? Buy them food! *(aside)* Such obstinacy!
Judah, you persuade him.

JACOB A female tongue
Is like the chattering of silly birds;
It has no weight, no depth. Dinah, go!
Tend the fires, the pots. Leave me in peace.

Exit Dinah as Jacob motions to his sons to help him stand. All three remain standing near him, looking towards him

JACOB *(to himself)* Dinah is tyrannical! How unlike
My Leah of the gentle eyes. (*sighs*) Judah,
She is right in what she says. I ought to act.
(*with despair*) How vulnerable is extreme old age!
(*swiftly*) Once I was a doughty man, a fighter.

In the womb I fought for the supremacy
With Esau, gripping Esau's *he*-el as
I thrust out into life. Then, when I was a man
I stole his birthright, offering him lentils for it
As he strode home famished from the hunt.
Last, when our father Isaac drew near death
I stole from Esau Isaac's dying blessing. How?
By putting hairy kid's fur on my neck
And hands, wearing Esau's reeking clothes.
Exploiting Isaac's blindness,
Resolutely, I usurped my brother's place.
How could God have used the heedless Esau for
His purposes? A smooth and base, conniving man
Like me was of more use because of my
Intensity. Yes, once I was a fighter.
Now, Judah, I am old, unrecognisable,
Decrepit in my body and my mind –
And all my life is centred on a fear,
The fear of losing Benjamin. It is – shaming.
(*briskly*) Return to Egypt, Judah. Buy the food we need.

JUDAH (*dryly*) And Benjamin goes with me?

JACOB (*in sudden anguish*) Ah! How can he?

JUDAH He *must* come with us. If – if Benjamin
Stays here with you the vizier will claim
We're foreign spies. We'll not return to Hebron.
There'll be bloodshed in Avaris. Here, you'll starve.

JACOB) *(angrily*) You told the man too much about us. Why?

JUDAH *(patiently)* To show him we were all one family
Of harmless shepherds, not the band of spies
He took us for. A hundred times we have
Described the terror he inspired, his threats
Of death if he should prove our guilt.
We could keep nothing hidden from his eyes –
All-seeing, penetrating eyes, that blazed
With fury – and expect his mercy.
And so we said we came to Egypt, in
Obedience to our father, only to buy food,
And that to keep our father company
The apple of his eye, his last born son,
Remained with him. We told the truth. What else?
Should we have died from seeming furtive?
Meanwhile our hostage waits for us and the
Supplies we need are with him in Avaris.
We'll bring you both. Send us with Benjamin.
The vizier, finding Benjamin with us,
Will have no reason for severity.
Eleven sons will come safe home to Hebron.

REUBEN Trust me, my father. I will bring him home.
I pledge the lives of my two sons. Take theirs
For his, if I should fail to bring him back.

JUDAH No, Reuben. All responsibility is mine
And we will keep him safe. I beg you, father, put
An end to this delay and send us south.
Bless all your sons and bless our journey.

JACOB *(with resignation)* Take him then, and gather gifts
to sweeten
The lord vizier's thoughts: Balm, honey, spices;
Almonds, pistachios; silver for the grain

You brought us and *will* bring. Make sure we pay.
The mystery of the gifts might still turn sour.
Approach the vizier with Benjamin.
Pray God will prompt him to be merciful,
So Benjamin, the other brother – all of you
Return to Hebron. As for me – if I am
Bereaved, I am bereaved.

Exit Jacob.

JUDAH There he goes. How hard a battle it has been
For Israel to bow his neck to the
Inevitable. Tear-tracks glistened on
His cheeks. His voice was choked, his body
shrunken in
Its misery.Why weren't we tolerant,
Those many years ago, of his excessive love
Of Joseph? – Envy made us devils!

LEVI (*angrily*) We let his love of Joseph stab a wound
in us,
And turned the dagger of it round and round
Inside, till we were maddened with the pain.

JUDAH We tore our father's life apart like famished wolves.
So – how did we become the men we were?

REUBEN (*thoughtfully*) It was inherent in our character.
The destroying was innate in us for years,
A dormant story waiting to be brought to life.
One day, we acted out the crime our shape
Had made *al*most inevitable: You, from hate;
And I, from negligence, caused by my lust.
(*nobly*) Are the evils in a human life

A system of Almighty Punishment
Or do they only stem from human character?
God permits us to choose error, if we wish.
As tiniest children we distinguish good
From evil. Grown to manhood we are free
To turn our back on goodness, if we choose.
Then every drama, every tragedy's
A crisscrossed inter-twining, a complicated knot
Of human sins; for which, in each year-long hour
Of our affliction, we blame God.

JUDAH (*swiftly*) If man were perfect, life would still
be tragic.
Always there'd be death and illness, all
The pains of our mortality; there'd
Be accidents, caused in all innocence,
And stormy convulsions of sea and earth
And air, in which no man is safe.
Yet, Reuben, you are right. Almost all
Life's anguish stems from man. Man is the cause.

REUBEN How many cruel centuries, how many
Thousands of barbaric years has man devoted
To destroying man! He's never solved
The problem of himself, nor ever will.
Though man's one physiology, one soul, one person,
Each moment, somewhere on this earth,
Foul man performs atrocities on man.
Every age we live in is the age of cruelty
And man is his own hell. – Brothers, in
These past few weeks we've felt new horror at
The wound we dealt our father, horror and
Remorse; remorse because we cut his Joseph from
His life; remorse because we gave him twenty years

Of fear – fear that Rachel's Benjamin
Might also die. – Ah yes, poor old man.

JUDAH Our great betrayal of the patriarch
Harmed all our lives and he would kill us if
He knew. If only that respect for him,
By which we set such store, had ruled us all,
That fatal day. (*resignedly*) Well, brothers, on with life!
We'll do the best we can.

LEVI (*cheerfully*) I see the women
Scurrying about, like mice disturbed
At harvest. Soon we shall be ready to depart.

REUBEN (*briskly*) To die perhaps in Egypt, or to live in jail.

JUDAH (*firmly*) Hoping to save our families, we'll run the risk.

SCENE V

A bustling street in the Egyptian Capital Avaris. Someone off-stage is playing a flute. Enter Intef.

INTEF (*out of breath*) I'll wait here at the gateway for the Hebrews
And lead them to their brother's villa.
I have a moment's respite – time to *think*. (*draws deep breath*)
How is mortal man to understand our vizier's mind?
I've been his steward nine years now and still
I find him disconcerting. Many brothers – ten –

Are trailing after with their donkeys.
And Benjamin has come, the vizier's
Full brother. – Have I witnessed scenes of glad
Reunion? No. Standing far away, the lord
Of Egypt stared as coolly as a sculptured sphinx,
Counted them, stared again, instructed me
To lead them here. Privately the vizier weeps
With yearning for his brothers. It seems
My lord has set himself a task and will not swerve
Till it is done. What task? And how? Who knows?
One thing is certain: There is wisdom in it.
If I discovered our Zathnath-Paneah is
The incarnation of our Ibis-headed Thoth
The god of wisdom, I'd feel no surprise.
Here come the vizier's ten brothers now –
The picture of dejection! I'll speak Hebrew.

Enter Judah, Reuben, Levi and, as Judah and Reuben converse on stage, Dan, Naphtali, Gad, Asher, Issachar, Zebulun and Benjamin. Off-stage donkeys bray and harness jingles.

JUDAH (*anxiously*) If the vizier has sent for us, perhaps
His purpose is to make us all his slaves
Because we made no payment for our grain.
Donkeys and all, this land may swallow us alive.
I am afraid.

REUBEN (*in an undertone, urgently*) The vizier's steward's waiting there.
This is the house.

JUDAH (*loudly, to Intef*) My lord, our being asked
To come here's a mistake. When last we bought

Some sacks of Delta grain, each brother paid
The granary the right amount, in silver.
Then on our homeward journey, opening
Our sacks, mysteriously we found in each
The silver we had paid. There was no theft!

REUBEN (*swiftly*) We need to buy more grain from you and so,
My lord, we've brought the silver for our fresh
Supplies *and* those we purchased earlier.
We are honest men – in money matters.

INTEF (*calmly*) Calm yourselves. The money tallied at
The granary. God put the silver in your sacks.
It was a gift. – I see another man approaching.
Gentlemen, would you recognise your brother?

Enter Simeon.

LEVI The question's idiotic.

INTEF Here is Simeon, whom
You have not seen for many months.

LEVI Simeon!

INTEF (*tonelessly*) Ah! So you *recognise* your brother!

SIMEON (*joyfully*) Levi, Judah, Reuben! I despaired of seeing you
Again.

LEVI What happened to you, Simeon?

SIMEON I lay in chains in prison, in a mood
Of black rebellion, devising ways
Of fighting those who came to feed me. They'd
Use truncheons they took out of cases to
Attack me as I rose to challenge them.

LEVI We guessed you would be harshly treated.

SIMEON I suppose they wore me down. My spirit
Weakened and was haunted by the past:
My slaughter of the Hivite princes,
Hamor, Shechem; all my other deeds of
Violence; the bitter set of Dinah's mouth
Worst of all, the face of Joseph loomed,
As though he were a hand's breadth from me,
Crouching on the earthen floor. You know
How close I came to stabbing him. – At last
I groaned aloud: 'Joseph, Hamor, Dinah, Shechem!'
When next I woke I saw the vizier,
Towering like a temple, staring down
At me. He said nothing, went away again.
I repudiated in my mind the acts
For which I'm infamous. The sorrow of
My spirit reached the air in troubled cries.

REUBEN (*in an undertone*) Can this be Simeon speaking, Judah?
Can a man like Simeon change?

SIMEON I was mortally
Ashamed of all this weakness till I understood
It was to God that I had yielded, not to man –
The God who made me as I am. The chains
Were struck from me – as though my thoughts had
been

The adze. I was given a pleasant room
Inside the prison, treated with respect.

JUDAH (*thoughtfully*) A most uncanny story.

INTEF (*authoritatively*) Gentlemen,
You'll dine with the lord vizier at noon.
Now follow me, and I will show you to a room,
Where you may wash your feet. Your donkeys will
Be cared for. (*joyfully*) Ah, here comes the vizier,
Zaphnath-Paneah!

Enter Joseph.

JOSEPH (*unemotionally*) So you have arrived.
Come, walk with me along the path. Are you well?

JUDAH (*humbly*) Yes, my lord. My lord, you speak good Hebrew now.

JOSEPH And your father? Is your father still alive?

JUDAH My lord, though very old, he is alive and well.

JOSEPH And this must be the youngest brother, whom
You mentioned.

JUDAH Yes, my lord. This is Benjamin,
Our father's favourite.

JOSEPH (*kindly*) Good. Benjamin,
My thanks to you for coming. Heaven bless you!
(*aside*) I must leave them all, and weep my fill.

INTEF Hebrews, follow me and I will show you where to go.

SCENE VI

A room in Joseph's house. Enter Joseph and Intef.

JOSEPH (*with verve*) Intef, my faithful steward, that was merry!

INTEF It was, my lord. Your brothers, who refuse
To know they are your brothers, heartily
Enjoyed themselves. You sat apart, of course,
As an Egyptian and an overlord.
The other men of Egypt ate in one group
And your Hebrews, separately, in another.

JOSEPH When they grew aware that they were seated
In the order of their birth, they were astounded.

INTEF (*laughs*)They looked so *mystified*!

JOSEPH With their eyes
They anxiously enquired of one another
What this meant and studied my impassive face.
'Coincidence', they thought at last. 'No-one knows
Our dates of birth.'

INTEF As one man, three brothers
Shrugged and drank their wine, to drown perplexity.

JOSEPH When you took them from my table portions of
Cooked meat, they were amazed to see you set
Before my brother, Benjamin, a mound
Five times the size of theirs.

INTEF So were the Hebrews' eyes –
Five times the normal size!

JOSEPH There ensued
Another pantomime of the investigating
Eyes; eyes popping out and swivelling,
Looking for a reason. Why would Benjamin,
To whom I'd spoken once, be valued more
Than all the rest? Again they made no headway
with
The riddle, gave up, then – forgot bewilderment,
Grew loud and jovial, full of laughter, following my
Example.

INTEF Yes, my lord, two blatant clues
You gave them all to your identity,
Making it as clear as day, teasing them
To recognise you as their brother.
They only saw – an alien Egyptian prince.

JOSEPH (*soberly*) The next move in this comedy is not a joke.
It brings a large fear, mercifully brief.
Intef, you will fill my brothers' sacks with grain;
Once more, place the silver that they pay you
In the sacks; but also – hide this silver goblet
In the youngest brother's sack, in Benjamin's.
Let them depart at daybreak, but before
They've travelled far, ride after them and ask them:
'Why do you repay our good with evil?'
Let your soldiers search their baggage, find
The cup, seize Benjamin. While my brothers wail,
Lament and tear their garments, see they load
Their donkeys. Lead them all back here to me –
And we shall see – what we shall see!

SCENE VII

The route to Canaan, a few hours' journey from Avaris. Sounds of donkeys, jingling harness and many men, off-stage. Enter Judah, and Reuben, who are in the rear of the brothers' caravan. Enter Intef, with soldiers, overtaking them.

INTEF (*thunderously*) Stop, Hebrews! Go no further!

REUBEN (*in astonishment*) The vizier's steward!

JUDAH (*boldly*) Ah! It's you. *Your* group was travelling in our wake
And gaining on us. – Intef, you've a message?

INTEF Soldiers, search the Hebrews' sacks!

Exit Soldiers.

JUDAH (*angrily*) Why? Why?
Why this insult?

INTEF (*with zest, enjoying his performance*) Why have you repaid
Our good with evil?

JUDAH (*taken aback*) I don't understand.

INTEF My lord the vizier's silver wine cup's missing.
You've repaid his hospitality with theft.

JUDAH (*vehemently*) I swear we haven't stolen it! (*stunned*) If by

Some devilry the cup has crept into
Our baggage, take my life! My despair
Is greater than my anger! How can we
Be thieves? Would thieves have asked you if
they owed
You mounds of coins? If you find it, kill me!

REUBEN (*firmly*) If the silver cup is found in our belongings,
Kill whoever has it and enslave the rest!

INTEF We know you have repaid our generosity
With criminality. You'll answer for
The crime – but only he who stole the cup
Shall be our slave. The others shall go free. Wait here!

Exit Intef.

JUDAH (*horrified*) When I turned and saw the billowing
dust clouds
Racing in pursuit – my heart plummeted,
Like a man who stumbles off a precipice.
'Wrong!' I thought. 'Can men who laugh with Egypt's
Vizier have enemies in Egypt?' –
Terror is the vizier's other name.
What a fool I was, to let myself be lulled! –
I'll see what Intef's men are doing,

Exit Judah.

REUBEN (*solemnly*) We were exulting in the thought of bringing
Benjamin safe home again from Egypt.
Alas, we are too guilty to be left in peace.
Little by little, our guilt has acquired its own
Identity: A vulture circling in the heavens

Above our heads, it falls continually from
The sky to pounce on us, and tear our lives
To pieces with its talons.

Enter Judah, Simeon and Levi.

JUDAH Reuben, it's
Uncanny! First they searched your sacks, then looked
In Simeon's, Levi's, mine and so on – everyone's
In order of his date of birth. Last comes
Benjamin, whose sacks they're searching now.

A sharp cry of despair is heard off-stage. Enter Intef and soldiers with Benjamin.

REUBEN It sounds as if they've found the cup we didn't steal.

INTEF Yes. Judah, we have found the thief! With
This silver goblet hidden in his robe,
He slunk out when our vizier dismissed you.

BENJAMIN That's
A lie! – It was in the sack without my knowledge!

JUDAH He is innocent!

INTEF (*icily*) I will have silence!
Our lord vizier has treated all
You men like brothers. In response, you stole!
Be silent in your shame!

The brothers utter murmurs and cries of anger.

REUBEN Simeon, did you steal

The cup and use it to incriminate him – out
Of jealousy?

SIMEON You incestuous lecher, I did not!
Aah! I could choke you!

REUBEN Try, you hamstringer
Of oxen!

JUDAH Silence, you two madmen! Where's
The sense in quarrelling among ourselves?
And given the presence of the vizier's silver
Goblet in our midst it's pointless to
Affirm our innocence. We are lost men!
Intef, I promised you a life. My life! Kill me!

INTEF How have you middle-aged fathers failed to learn
That only honesty is safe? Elementary
Prudence should have kept light fingers from the silver.

SIMEON I shall die of rage!

REUBEN And I, of fear for Benjamin.

INTEF The vizier is not a cruel man.
He will not punish all of you. Only the thief
Shall be his slave. The rest shall keep their freedom.

JUDAH (*in despair*) What a calamity! Returning without
Benjamin, my brothers, how could we
Endure the sight and sound of Israel's grief?
I could howl like an animal in
My wretchedness. (*eagerly*) Reuben, we must offer
To be slaves instead of Benjamin.

BENJAMIN (*protesting*) Why sacrifice yourselves for me?

JUDAH Chiefly to save our father, Benjamin.
Because *you*, above all, are innocent –
That too; but chiefly for our father Jacob's sake.

INTEF (*with authority*) You must return with me to Avaris.

JUDAH Disastrous day! We are like men who
Saw the lightning strike the ground before them,
Stunned and blinded by the searing shock-wave.

ACT IV

THE HEALING

SCENE I

A room in Joseph's villa in Avaris. Joseph is sitting on a dais in a chair with carved arms. Enter Intef and guards, escorting Joseph's brothers.

INTEF — My lord, I have compelled the guilty Hebrews to
Return with me to Avaris. Your lordship's cup,
Which has the jackal-god engraved within the bowl –
Divine Anubis – had been taken by
The youngest.

JOSEPH — (*with zest*) O folly of mankind,
Always expecting to *profit* by its sin!
What have you done? You might have known a man
Like me would practise Divination. Can misdeeds
Be hidden from the supernatural eye?

JUDAH — (*wearily*) My lord, what shall we say? Can we prove
Our innocence? God has found out our sin.
Enslave us.

JOSEPH — (*briskly*) God forbid I should enslave
You all! Only one of you, the thief,

Shall be my slave. Leave him here. The rest
Of you, return to Canaan, to your father.
That is my decision. – Go in peace.

JUDAH (*kneels*) Hear me, my lord! Wrath must seem justified,
Because the cup was found with us, but do
Not let your anger flame against such wretches as
Ourselves – you who are as powerful
As Egypt's king. In all humility
I beg you: Listen to me!

JOSEPH (*coldly*) The brother who
Is guilty is my slave – his the larceny,
His the punishment. Be silent! Leave my
Presence and this land. Take your thieving customs back
To where they came from!

JUDAH *(distraught)* Hear your servant as he kneels!
How shall I deny what circumstances prove
Against us? In denial there's no hope.
One life is ruined. Lord of Egypt, let
That life be mine! Take my life for Benjamin's.

JOSEPH (*austerely*) You may present your reasons.

JUDAH My lord vizier,
In mercy take my life for his. He is
The youngest, born when Jacob had already reached
Old age. His mother's only other son,
Our father thinks, was slaughtered by a predator.
Jacob cannot live without his Rachel's one
Surviving son. In obedience to you,

My lord, we brought him out of Canaan. Each
Day now our father's life is shadowed by
His fear, his trembling fear for Benjamin.
My lord, the two men breathe one breath. The threads
Of their inseparable lives are intertwined.
Believe me: If our father sees our little
Caravan returning home and finds
The youngest is not there, the horror of
The loss will break his heart. Swiftly, through
A sudden stroke, or slowly, as a living wreck,
My loving father Israel will die
Of his son's absence. I could not bear
To see our father's misery; 'Trust me!'
I urged my father. 'He will come safe home.'
Lord vizier – my life for Benjamin's liberty!
I implore you to accept it. I will call
Down blessings on your head in all the years
I serve you, for this act of mercy.

JOSEPH (*warmly*) Judah, my Judah! – A noble offer,
Nobly spoken.

JUDAH (*startled*) You called me by my name?

JOSEPH (*rising to his feet*) My servants, and my steward, leave the room.

Exeunt Intef and guards.

(*controlled*) Judah, rise from your knees! Forgive my tears.
I cannot keep them back. The dam has burst.
My heart is hammering in my breast.

Why do you stare? Don't you recognise me?
Do you still not know me? Who else, in this
Foreign land, besides yourselves, can know
The order of your births? Can't you guess?
Have you forgotten the prophecy of the dream?
Whose whereabouts don't you know? Which of you
Vanished? Is it still not obvious? Look at me,
Closely. Can't you see that I am Joseph?

The brothers gasp in astonishment.

Yes, I am Joseph. I am alive. (*He weeps loudly then continues with a trace of tears in his voice*)
No wonder you are staring at me.
I am not coherent. My head is in
A whirlwind of past agony and present joy;
I can do nothing but shed torrents
And torrents of my tears. Come closer.
Do you wonder that my manner's strange?
How many years I've waited, longing for
You all, and yearning for reunion with
My family! And is my father Jacob still
Alive? Are you still speechless? Is there nothing
You can say to me, you tribe of Jacob's
Sons – my own full brother Benjamin?
Come nearer. Please don't stand so far away.

JUDAH (*politely*) My lord, we are your obedient servants.

JOSEPH Look at me more closely. Try to recognise
The seventeen-year-old alive in this –
Maturity. Look closely, Benjamin!
I am your brother Joseph. Reuben, look
At me – and Zebulun! Yes, you sold me

Into slavery. Who else would know
But Joseph, after all these years? You threw
Me down the well. You sold me to the Ishmaelites,
The merchants travelling to Egypt. – I am Joseph!
(*he weeps loudly*)

JUDAH (*deeply moved*) If you are Joseph, then my spirit is
More troubled than before. We did not steal,
Yet bear an incubus of guilt, as high
And rugged as Mount Sinai, guilt as black
As bitumen. How shall I, Judah, crushed
Beneath this weight of sin, look Joseph in the face?
If you are Joseph – dearly my soul longs
To find this true – then in my shame I may
Not raise my eyes to yours.

ZEBULUN (*passionately*) If you are Joseph, how
Can we approach you? The harm we did you sets
A barrier between us.

JOSEPH (*lovingly*) Brothers, all
My brothers, whose dear company I've yearned for, all
The days of all the years we have been kept apart, –
Forget you sold me. Never grieve again
At what you did. It was God who let
Your hearts be hardened, God who sent me into
Egypt to save Israel in the years of famine.
My brothers, how long have I waited! (*he weeps loudly*)

BENJAMIN (*astonished*) Joseph died – was killed – when I was still
A boy. Can Joseph come back from the dead?

JUDAH (*bravely*) Benjamin, we lied. He did not die.

BENJAMIN (*vexed*) How shall I understand a word of this?

JUDAH All of us but Reuben jointly sold
Your brother Joseph, your full brother, as a slave.
We were jealous of our father's love for him.

REUBEN (*hastily*) I also failed the boy.

BENJAMIN (*in horror*) How could you live
With such an act?

JUDAH (*sourly*) By smothering memory.

JOSEPH (*kindly*) Judah, do not grieve at what you did;
And Benjamin, don't look at them askance.
God's mercy for his Israel in the time
Of hunger placed me here in Egypt.

JUDAH (*bitterly*) Say rather: God devised a way to make
A good from our perversity.

JOSEPH (*soothingly*) Judah, Judah, God has made me like
A father to his majesty the king,
Who delegates all power to me. Take back
This message to our father: These are Joseph's
words:
"God has made me overlord of Egypt.
Come swiftly with our family and herds
To live in Egypt, close to Joseph, who
Will feed and cherish you." I am Joseph.
(*a sob*) Yes,
Yes – you can see it *now*. Tell my father of

My glory. Bring him! Hold me, Benjamin. (*they embrace*)
My brothers, pardon all my tears!

BENJAMIN I've ten
Sons, Joseph – more than all the rest – and Jacob
Calls them 'Rachel's grandsons'.

JOSEPH And Manasseh
Is my first -born son who taught me to forget
All those I loved in Canaan. Ephra*im*
We named the second, since he proved me
Fertile in this foreign land. My wife is
An Egyptian priestess. Judah, is our mother
Leah still alive?

JUDAH No. She's mourned
By Jacob as a paragon. Dinah. who
Inherits her authority, he brands a tyrant,
Claiming everything conspires to vex him.
What happened to you, Joseph, after villains sold you?

JOSEPH In Egypt *dreaming* of a well foretells
Imprisonment; so perhaps it's not
Surprising . . .

Enter Usher, with Khyan hard on his heels.

USHER His majesty the king!

Joseph's brothers gasp in awe and fall to their knees, bowing their heads.

KH'YAN Rise to your feet. Rise. I have come for
One moment's informality. We have

Waited many years, Zaphnath-Paneah
And I, to see you here in Egypt.
It is my joy to bid you welcome.
Zaphnath-Paneah, my courtiers and I
Have heard your violent sobs. Far to the south
They will have carried, all along the highway of
The Nile, to the tomb of great Osiris in
His city Abydos. Even Aswan may have heard
A murmur. Yes, your storm of tears has been
A second inundation. Yet we know these tears
Reve*al* utmost joy. I bring a message
To you from myself and from my courtiers:
We share in your rejoicing. We too weep tears
Of gladness for you all. So good has come
At last from hatred that lay hidden in
A smile, venomous as a hooded cobra by
The yellow blossom of the acacia.
Poison has turned to honey. This is
My message to my vizier's brothers: Come
To Egypt! Live in Egypt!

JOSEPH (*to his brothers*) You see? The king's
Provided wagons laden with provisions,
Held in readiness for your departure.
Return to Canaan swiftly. Bring our father here.
Transport your goods, your wives and children in
The wagons. Everything you leave behind
Will be replaced from Egypt's best.
Driving your flocks and herds before you,
Come down into Egypt.

KHYAN All of this
Has royal approval. Do not underestimate
This relative of yours because you know him.

He is the swivel bolt on which the door
Of Egypt turns. No man in all my Realm
Moves hand or foot unless this man permits it.
And so, my vizier, the gaping wounds
Of grief are closed with balm and soothing
Linen. I will leave you now.

JOSEPH Your majesty,
Accept our heartfelt gratitude!

Exeunt Khyan and Usher.

Benjamin,
I long to see our father!

REUBEN (*in an undertone*) So pensive, Judah?

JUDAH (*in an undertone*) Reuben, I am thinking of inevitable
Consequences. First we must convince
Our father Joseph is alive and then – and then
We have to make a full confession. (*a sotto voce groan*)

REUBEN (*in an undertone*) Rejoice with all your heart!

JUDAH (*in an undertone*) I do, I do!

JOSEPH (*loudly*) Beloved brothers, to the feast! I'll lead the way.

SCENE II

Jacob's Camp in Hebron. Jacob is surrounded by all eleven sons.

REUBEN Support the old man! He is fainting with the shock.

JACOB How can Joseph be alive? Twenty years ago
I saw his garment drenched in blood – his blood.
It struck my heart as sharp a blow as did
My dying Rachel, lying white and cold
As I held new-born Benjamin. My son
Alive? My head reels. Don't torment me.
My ancient sorrow for my son's a safe
Companion. Its cutting edge is dulled.
It is familiar. Leave me with it.

BENJAMIN (*joyfully*) The vizier knows the history of our family –
And secrets of my youth I only shared with Joseph.
Believe me, father, *he is* Joseph!
Who else would single out your youngest son?
Three hundred silver pieces and five times
As many clothes he's given me!

JACOB (*perplexed*) Bewildering.
I cannot take this in.– How shall I
Believe a son of mine rules Egypt?

JUDAH This – stranger – was so glad to see us all
He drowned us all in floods of tears, asking:
'Is my father Jacob still alive? What of
Our mother, Leah?' He sends ten donkeys
Laden with Egyptian presents for you,

All to be turned round again to amble
With us on our journey back to Egypt.

JACOB I am stupefied. I am slow. This is
A difficult idea.

JUDAH 'Bring our father south
To Egypt now,' said Egypt's vizier.
'I will be a shelter for our Israel
In the next five years of famine. You shall
Graze your flocks in Goshen. Don't quarrel on
The way. Behave yourselves!' *He* knows us.

BENJAMIN Joseph spoke of Rachel, our dead mother,
As we said goodbye. Lastly: 'Describe to Israel,'
He said, 'The princely ceremonial of
My life in Egypt, tell of the magnificence
Of everything I wear and own. Joseph,
Now first lord of Egypt, has the power to
Protect him.'

ZEBULUN There are massive ox-drawn wagons
Sent by Egypt's king, for us to bring
Our children, our possessions and our wives
Along the route of the oases into Egypt.
What you cannot bring, the king of Egypt
Will replace from Egypt's best.

JACOB (*sharply*) Wagons! Ah!
You *couldn't have bought* wagons!

JUDAH Joseph sends
Them to you on the orders of the king.

JACOB (*understanding at last*) The wagons! Only one of *us*, a man
Devoted to our tribe, would send them.
The wagons I can see with my own eyes.
You say they come from Joseph, from my son?

REUBEN From him.

JACOB (*filled with awe*) It is a miracle. My Joseph
Is alive. No sweeter words were ever heard.
You have found my vanished son alive,
My dear, dear son. It is a gift from Heaven.
I will journey down to Egypt, where
My son the mighty vizier awaits.
I'll see my living son before I die. –
Hurry, hurry. Make ready. Don't stand there.
(shouts) Dinah! Dinah! All of you, prepare
To journey down to Egypt, to my son!

SCENE III

Jacob's temporary Camp at Beersheba. It is night. A camp fire is visible and a tent or two. Enter from several directions all of Jacob's sons who are with him on the journey excepting Benjamin – all of them from Reuben to Zebulun.

REUBEN (*whispering urgently*) We must tell Israel now! Judah, Levi, what's
The use of travelling through the country like
A funeral cortège, weighed down by words
That must be said. The quiet evening is
Benign, serene. Tell our father now.

LEVI He'll utter lion's roars and use his knife.
The peaceful evening will be one of blood
And rage the moment he has understood.
Reuben, if in Egypt Joseph pleads with him
To spare us, Jacob may not seek revenge.

JUDAH (*incredulously*) So our victim is to beg our father
Not to hate us! Counsel of cowardice! (*firmly*)
Levi, we've a debt to pay. We can't avoid it.
Tell him at Beersheba, here and now.
We are leaving Canaan's geography behind.
Leave Canaan's evils here in Canaan.

REUBEN He agrees with me.

JUDAH Last night our father burnt
A sacrificial offering on the Altar here,
Looking for a sign to justify our
Great Migration into Egypt. In the night
He dreamed God spoke. Israel is confident,
At peace. We'll tell him now. But here he comes.
Draw aside and watch him from the shadows.

Enter Jacob.

JACOB (*thoughtfully*) Though we leave our land, our
God is always with us.
My vision at Beersheba is as great
A blessing as the vision of the ladder up
To heaven at Luz. There I saw ascending and
Descending angels and God promised to
Be with me in my years between the Tigris and
Euphrates. Last night, in my vision at
The Well of Isaac's Vow, God promised He'll

Watch over us in Egypt and will lead us back
To Canaan, *still* the Promised Land. My cup
Is full, for by some miracle I journey now
To meet my long-dead son – who's raised to life.
I buried Joseph's bloodstained robe, through which
His blood had seeped in twenty places – and yet –
He's here on earth, alive, a man of power,
Lord vizier of Egypt! Never mind
The mystery. My son was dead and is
Alive again. God knows, it is enough!

JUDAH Father!

JACOB Judah? You here? And the rest,
Emerging from the dark. Why are you
Conferring here at this hour?

JUDAH Father, we'll
Explain to you how Joseph disappeared.

JACOB Surely only Joseph can do that. (*astonished*) Judah, in
The flickering firelight you look aghast!

JUDAH Father, I am dying of my.shame!

JACOB Dan, Asher, Zebulun – all of you
Look anxious. Why? You should rejoice.Your
Brother's resurrected from the dead.

JUDAH Our gratitude for his survival fills our lives
With sweetness. We are murderers whose victim
Is alive. God forgive me. Father, pardon me.
You'll need to punish all of us but Benjamin.

JACOB (*angrily*) Murderers? Have you done to death another
Shechem and another Hamor? Need I know?
Must I listen to another of your horrible
Confessions? After I have spent so many
Blighted years, must you ruin all my joy?

JUDAH (*steadily*) Father, we made Joseph disappear.

JACOB (*stares at him in shock*)

JUDAH (*steadily*) We sent our brother out of Canaan.

JACOB (*feebly*) My heart is weak, my hearing fails me.
Words . . .
I hear the echo of your words, and every head is
bowed.
(*softly* Your younger brother . . . Why, in heaven's
name?

JUDAH (*firmly*) Envy. Hatred. Wrath. Because you
idolised him.

JACOB (*horrorstruck)* Why was there so much blood?
What did you do?.
You stabbed him?

JUDAH No, it wasn't Joseph's blood.
Debating whether we should kill the boy,
We saw a merchant caravan, a caravan
Of Ishmaelites, and sold him as a slave.

JACOB (*tonelessly*) You thought of fratricide.

JUDAH We did, but in the event
The blood was goat's blood.

JACOB (*with growing anger*) You sold Joseph as
A slave, to live or die alone!

JUDAH That is what we did.

JACOB Then all these barren years I might have had
His company. You gave me years of needless grief.

JUDAH That is so.

JACOB *(in horror)* What sort of creatures are you?

JUDAH (*briskly*) Devils, now and then. Not always.

JACOB Judah! And
I thought you so much nobler than the rest.
How could you do it?

JUDAH I had the strength to stop it – and I laughed,
I saw Joseph's tears and laughed. That is why
I'm spokesman now. My guilt it greatest.

JACOB (*furiously*) I concur. As your stature is, so is
your guilt.
You're the greatest scorpion of them all!

JUDAH (*cut to the quick*) True!

JACOB What a family have I fathered!
Ten of you stung me with your scorpions' tails,
And, callous, watched the poison flowing through
My veins to numb my heart. You saw my agony
And were not moved. From the fortress of your
Hatred you looked out dry-eyed. And at Joseph's

Sufferings, his fear and helpless desperation,
At your brother's misery, you laughed!

JUDAH (*dryly*) Only Reuben loved the boy as he deserved.
He planned to save him surreptitiously
And take him home, missed the crucial time and,
When he heard the boy was sold, wanted to
Pursue the caravan and buy him back.
In vain. – We kept tight hold of Joseph's price.

JACOB How have you not drowned in your own evil?

JUDAH For many years we did not know what we
Had done – thinking ourselves justified.
Alas, we understand at last and are
Appalled at what we did.

JACOB (*slowly, as he wrestles with his thoughts*) If anything
Could teach me how to hate you, it would be
Your barbarism to my son. (*as in a dream*) I loved him for
His mother's sake, Rachel, who died near Bethlehem.
My Rachel! Never was there soul more loved
Or soul more loving. All day long I laboured,
And in the quiet evening came to you,
The haven of my peace. Rested and refreshed,
We left the earth behind and flew on eagles' wings,
Aspiring, travelling as high as mind
Could reach. You taught me what to be. What a thorn
In your dear flesh – your tainted love of Leah,
Your so fertile sister! You bore Joseph
After years of bitter failing to conceive.

Oh my love, you died so long ago!
My Rachel was a cooling breeze, showering
Scented blossoms round my head.
{looking at each of his sons in turn)
As for Joseph, her dear son and mine,
I have not seen him with these eyes for twenty
years.
So – what do I feel for you, my sons who took
From me my son? I cannot hate you.
I find I love you still. All of you
Are my own flesh. You spring from joys and loves
Of Israel's youth. How shall a father not
Forgive his flesh and blood, conceived in love.
(*solemnly*)
You are sacrosanct in my paternal love.
Be terrorists, assassins if you choose.
Murder one another. I shall mourn the dead,
But never fail to love my living sons who feel
Remorse for evil past. Look what Simeon did
At Shechem city, yet I love him. Suddenly
I find I have ten Simeons. My heart
Is sore and I am wounded by your guilt.
Yet all of you – I love. Whatever hideous thing
You may have done, you are my sons, whom I
Shall always love. You think that I say this
Because my Joseph is alive. If he were dead,
And by your hand, I'd not unsay one word.

JUDAH *(utters a groan)* It is not right that we should meet
with so
Much mercy. Punish us!

JACOB (*firmly*) You are forgiven.
My love of you was always absolute.

Will you need me to protect you from
Our Joseph?

REUBEN Malice never was a part of him.

JUDAH When he had finished weeping tears
Of joy on all our shoulders, we were drenched.
And all the time we felt the burning aura of
His love. He was like a day of sun
And showers. Joseph loves us.

SIMEON (*fiercely*) No! Fear Joseph!
I say: Fear him! Joseph laughed with us, he
Wept with us, he terrorised us all by turns.
For days we lay expecting execution, like
Assassins caught red-handed. Joseph has
A tyrant's instability. What will he do next?
He is the ruler of a long thin land,
An isolated land, winding through
The heart of endless deserts. We shall be
Dependent on his mercy. Think! If I
Were Joseph, there'd be wailing wives and dull
Eyed, hungry boys in every tent but Benjamin's.
Their fathers I'd see chained up by the neck –
Lashed with whips; labouring in the darkness of
A mine – till, after years in which they'd never seen
The sky, they died. Why spare men such as we are,
Creatures of dung, for whom vindictive vengeance is
Instinctive, seldom curbed, almost thought of as
A duty showing manly courage? *He* said he
Forgave me, yet I saw a strange light
Gleaming in his eye.

JUDAH (*soberly*) You saw his tears, his tears.
(*swiftly*) It *was* odd, I admit. He did not say:
'My brothers, look at me! This vizier is
Your Joseph'. True. Instead he let us fear
Him, till we had returned with Benjamin
A second time. Why? Who knows? It is
A mystery. Believe me, Jacob, Simeon,
He was an actor when he frowned and threatened
– and
We quailed before his rank and power but,
When Joseph wept and said how much he loved us,
His every word and tear were truth.

JACOB (*with composure*) Thank you, Judah.
You're the wisest here. If now and then
A sudden fear assails Jacob's sons,
It is because of guilt. If there is ever need,
I shall protect you from my son, but there
Will be no need. I trust him. But for surface
Squabbles of the everyday, our nomad
City in the east of Egypt will be tranquil –
No torn hearts, no torn lives. It will not be
The least of Joseph's monuments. Meanwhile
I swear to you, for me, the past is past.
Bygones are bygones. Lightened of the past,
We'll travel into Egypt, to our glad
Reunion with my son. My son was lost
And now is found. My son was dead and is
Alive again. My cup of joy is full.

SCENE IV

A room in Joseph's villa, with a water jar on a stand. Enter Joseph and Judah.

JOSEPH (*excitedly*) We'll leave at once – to meet my father, Judah!

JUDAH Steady, brother! I must eat – and talk to you.

JOSEPH Forgive me, Judah. Here you stand dust-covered, tired
From many weeks of journeying from Hebron,
Topped by rushing to me from my father's camp
In Goshen, and – and I forget to offer food
And wine! I'll send a servant to the kitchens. (*claps hands*)

Enter servant to receive Joseph's command and exit instantly.

Bring food and wine.(*to Judah*) We'll travel in an hour.

JUDAH And now you'll spare me several moments of
Your time. I've dark suspicions of my younger
Brother, the manipulator, of
The man who makes men dance to all his tunes.

JOSEPH (*coolly*) Here, meanwhile, is the water jar. (*handing it to him*)

JUDAH (*contrite*) Ah! I remember offering you a water jar,
At Dothan, many aeons ago.
(Draws in breath through his teeth) And then,
We threw you in the well.

JOSEPH Now, as to your
Dark suspicions, Judah – they are the screen
You build to hide from you your growing feeling of
Humiliation – at the dance you danced.
(*lovingly*) You know the reasons, Judah.

JUDAH (*gives a deep sigh*) I'm a simple man.

JOSEPH (*ironically*) Hm. really?

JUDAH (*briskly*) Right! It wasn't possible
For you, encountering us after two
Decades, to say without preamble: 'I am Joseph'.

JOSEPH (*briskly*) Of course it was a possibility.
I nearly did it. It is what my blood cried out for.

JUDAH (*rapidly, angry with himself*) How lightly we'd
have taken it! 'Well, well.
So fortune favoured you! Surely you'll
Not sulk because we sold you? Only twelve
Short years of slavery and imprisonment?
A bagatelle! Fancy meeting you!
It only goes to show the world is small.'

JOSEPH (*laughs*) Quite right! You would have skimmed
across the top,
Ten sidewinder vipers sketching hieroglyphs
Across the sands.

JUDAH Well now – so instead
Of saying; 'I'm Joseph', you reduced us to
The extremity of terror – a far cry from
Embracing us, now wouldn't you say? So we,
Your fine, intrepid brothers, men proverbial for
Heroic valour – several in Canaan
Call it something worse – we band of brothers shook
Like aspen leaves, changing colour as
We quivered. Joseph, does this action square
With bearing no ill-will? There now – it's out!

JOSEPH (*cheerfully*) Why, so it is!

JUDAH Well – what's your answer then?

JOSEPH My answer is – some food and wine for you
Before we see our father.

JUDAH Is that all
The satisfaction I'm to get?

JOSEPH The Delta wine's
Particularly good.

JUDAH (*ironically*) Thank you, little brother!

JOSEPH So tell me all about our father, Judah.

SCENE V

Jacob's Camp in Goshen. Enter Joseph and Dinah from different directions.

JOSEPH (*excitedly*) Aren't you my sister Dinah?

DINAH (*hesitantly*) Are you – (*joyfully*) Joseph?
I can't believe it. Heavenly! (*They embrace.*)

JOSEPH My dear.

DINAH My brother, how I've missed you. *(laughs)* We are both
A little older. But what splendour! You
Have driven a chariot from Avaris – is that right?

JOSEPH Yes. Judah brought me word. Is Jacob here?
Where is he?

DINAH Jacob saw the chariots.
He's making ready. Joseph, finding you
Alive in Egypt makes me count my life
A happy one! Ah, here comes our father.
I will guide him to you.

Enter Jacob.

JACOB (*unsteadily*) Dinah, Dinah,
Who is this? Who is this Egyptian Prince,
This lord who condescends to talk to you?

DINAH (*joyfully*) Come father, come to him. Look closely.

JACOB Made-up eyes, Egyptian hair-cut, golden
Necklace, jewelled ornamental chains
And pectorals, white linen, such an air
Of wielding a divine authority –
Why should so high a being talk to you?
Who is this man?

DINAH Look closely, father.

JACOB (*overwhelmed*) Can this man really be my Joseph?
(*with great emotion*)
There are tears in his Egyptian eyes!

JOSEPH (*through his tears*) O father, bless your son!

JACOB You are my *son*.
Don't kneel down. Embrace me. I am overcome.
If you do not hold me I shall fall.
I am dazed. I see a face so dearly loved,
And yet so changed – my *living* Joseph.

JOSEPH Father!

JACOB Joseph, you were such a loss – a loss
I could not stand. And now you hold me in your arms,
Crushing my ribs enough to crack them,
Crushing to death the misery of the past!

JOSEPH (*gives a sob*) Ah, Jacob!

JACOB (*overwhelmed*) What an honour for an ordinary
Shepherd, an Egyptian Prince who folds

Him in his arms – and weeps and weeps! (*sadly*) I saw
You stride away when you were seventeen
And never guessed that you were leaving my
Most wretched life.

JOSEPH (*controlled, but with the trace of tears in his voice*)
Inside the well, below
The ground, half dead, I lay in terror, hour
By *ho*ur, of the worst that man can do.
At last they sold me. Simeon and Levi's tongues
Passed delicately over grinning lips
While Judah, laughing with his eyebrows at
My price, rubbed forefinger on thumb. They
Were merry, as if – shearing sheep. For weeks
And months I was a madman, knowing you
Believed me dead.

JACOB The waters of the well
Of misery will drain away at last
And every drop will vanish in the timeless sand.
My dear son, I have seen you living, after
Twenty years. It is enough. I have
No more to ask of life. I am content to die.

Enter Judah and Reuben, who stand and watch from well outside Joseph and Jacob's field of vision.

JOSEPH My long lost father, we'll be granted time together.

JACOB These few moments are enough, an everlasting feast,
A bliss that *he*als all the wounds of old.
My son, our grief was of this world, no deeper
Than the ocean, while our joy, our joy –
Is timeless singing in the fields of stars
Before the throne of God.

JOSEPH Ah, Jacob!

JACOB It was your brother Benjamin who saved me.
His love became more visible to me
When you had gone. He waited patiently
For me to be consoled because he lived.
Each day he'd crouch beside me as I grieved.
Our love grew deeper, strongly bonded by
Our love for you.

JUDAH (*in an undertone*) And so we see two men
Together after twenty years apart.
Which man received the greater injury?
I, Judah, maimed both lives. I am a rogue.

REUBEN (*in an undertone*) Be comforted. A crowd of men must bear
The blame for rushing headlong where they knew
They should not go. But all is now made good.
Come, and leave them to their bliss.

JUDAH I need
To hear them both, in concert, say I am
Forgiven. Leave me here.

Exit Reuben.

JACOB More tears, my son?

JOSEPH (*controlled*) Of joy at our reunion, that I
Have longed for since I was at Dothan, all
Those years ago. I've yearned for you since then
And feared there could be no reunion in
This life.

JACOB Yet here we are together in
This foreign land and I'll be happy as
I die. My burial arrangements . . .

JOSEPH (*interrupting, soothingly*) Can
Be thought of later.

JACOB You are saddened at
My weakness, conscious you are powerless
Against my death, so listen to my plans.
You must fulfil my wishes.

JOSEPH (*almost laughing*) Jacob!

JACOB Take my body to the cave at Machpelah,
To let me rest by Abraham and Sarah,
Isaac and Rebecca, and my Leah.

JOSEPH (*soberly*) It shall be done. Egyptian mourners in
Their chariots will escort you after seventy days
Of mourning.

JACOB (*briskly*) Joseph! Joseph, you'll stay here –
Your bones must stay – until the time for
Exodus has come; – and then, of course,
You'll travel back to Canaan. When you think
I'm dying, bring me Ephraim and Manasseh, your
Two sons. My dying blessing is reserved
For them, to reaffirm that they belong
With Israel, not Egypt. Now my mind's
At peace and death is welcome.

JUDAH (*loudly, urgently, as he approaches*) Jacob! Joseph!
Jacob, Joseph, what of me, the architect
Of all your misery?

JACOB You are forgiven
A thousand times!

JOSEPH Embrace us, Judah.

JUDAH Instead I *kneel* to you. Let me crawl
Through life on raw and bleeding knees until
I have atoned. Give me penance after penance!

JACOB No, Judah. Rise, my son.

JUDAH Your eyes are full
Of unshed tears. If you two are mere men,
Then what is God? Certainly not less! Does God,
Watching the sinner and the sinned against,
Watching the smirched soul, with its earthly
Victim of the broken heart or broken
Body; does God weep giant tears for both?
Is God a river of great crystal tears?
And is this the only punishment, in
Earth or heaven – to understand the man
I am and what I've done? Is hell absolute
Self-knowledge, laid bare by the blinding light
Of holiness? Dear brother and dear father,
My distress is great!

JACOB Judah, come to us.

They embrace one another.

JUDAH Noble, noble hearts! And Joseph, please
Forgive my asking for a sop to my
Reviving pride, now crushed once more.

JOSEPH (*winningly*) Forgive *me*, Judah.

JUDAH For what? For cleansing us, so we could build
On truth? Willingly! We came at last.
You saw men hard of heart who years ago
Had told themselves their sins were justified.
Our consciences were silted up. You –
Dealt harshly with yourself, with us, for all
Our sakes and, as you healed us, turned aside to weep.
We too have wept and our remorse is stored
In jars of tears. One day the vessels we have filled
Will counterweigh our guilt and we'll be whole.
My second youngest brother – well, what shall
I say? It's simple.There's no doubt at all.
His greatness . . .

JOSEPH (*roundly*) He is cut out of the rainbow of
The seven deadly sins, but does the best he can.
For one thing more he humbly asks forgiveness.

JUDAH Ah! The terror of the cup!

JOSEPH Consider.
What resulted? When I incriminated
Benjamin, all of you, – and Judah, *you* above
All – offered up your lives for him, laid them down
To spare our father grief: Finding the
Pathway out of the Labyrinth, unwinding all
The cruelty, the slavery and grief
You dealt out long ago. You – were filled
With pity! Tears stand in my eyes and will,
Throughout my life, whenever I remember
How you showed your overpowering urge
To absolute self-sacrifice. Try, after that,
To tell yourselves that you are evil men!
Therefore I say: Giant Judah, noble Judah –
Forgive me and – think better of yourself!

JACOB (*with sober joy*) Could a man have finer sons?
And one
Of them is known in all the world as vizier
Of Egypt. My own son is vizier
Of Egypt! He's a prince who lives in palaces
Of gold and drives great golden chariots, wheels
Of thunder, spinning whirlwinds, hurtling onward.
As I saw you reach the camp I did
Not dare to guess that that celestial,
Shining warrior, darting rays of gold
Through clouds of dust, was Jacob's son. To see
How you are honoured now rewards me for
My years of loss, which I cannot regret
Now that I know that they have made of you
A man of destiny, the mighty man who rules
All Egypt on behalf of Egypt's king.
How strange, the fate of Rachel's first born son!
What joy, to see my lovely Rachel's boy
Supremely blest.

JUDAH (*after a slight pause, gravely*) As are we all.

JACOB Once joy reigns, all sorrow fades, an unreal dream

JOSEPH When once you've rested, my dear Canaanites,
We're all to have an audience with the king,
Who's like a son to me. He'll bid you welcome and
Confirm where you may always live – not far
From me. And so we are together.

JACOB It is a miracle, a story of great beauty.
I'm tiring now, my Joseph. Take me to
My tent and sit with me until I sleep.

SCENE VI

A Hall in the royal palace at Avaris. Enter Khyan with Ushers and Fan-bearers. Enter Joseph with Jacob, followed by Benjamin, Judah, Dan, Gad and Zebulun, then Reuben, Simeon, Levi, Naphtali, Asher and Issachar.

JOSEPH (*briskly*) Your majesty, my father has arrived
In Egypt with my brothers and their families.
First Benjamin and Judah, Dan and Gad
And Zebulun, approach to thank your majesty.
My father Israel will sit a moment on
This folding stool, to catch his breath.
And here are Reuben, Simeon and Levi,
Naphtali and Asher, lastly Issachar.

All except Jacob prostrate themselves before Pharaoh, then rise to a kneeling position.

KHYAN Rise to your feet, my friends! We've waited
Patiently for all your burly, bearded forms
To come and claim the space allotted you
In our Egyptian scene. Welcome! Welcome!

JUDAH (*soberly*) You've saved our lives by offering us a refuge.
We thank your majesty with all our hearts.

KHYAN It is a small repayment of the giant debt
I owe the saviour of my Two Lands of
The Reed and Lily. Which is Benjamin?

BENJAMIN I am Benjamin, your majesty.

KHYAN How remarkable your mother must have been;
A lady who could teach a boy – and make of him
A Joseph! Benjamin, pray tell me of your tribe.

BENJAMIN We are herdsmen – tending sheep and goats
And cattle – herdsmen, as our ancestors have been
For countless generations.

KHYAN (*thoughtfully*) Sheep you have,
Vast flocks of sheep. Then definitely you
Must settle now (if 'settle' is a word
That nomads use) in grazing land in Goshen to
The east. Do not go south to where Ram-headed
Khnum
Is worshipped as the sun.You'll be abhorrent to
The followers of Khnum, since you kill sheep –
And yet Khnum's devotees kill crocodiles,
Which The Fayum in worship decks with earrings of
Carnelian or chalcedony. Good!
Zaphnath-Paneah will see if some of you
Should serve as royal herdsmen. Live with peace
Of mind in Egypt, for my vizier's sake.
Zaphnath-Paneah, has Israel recovered?

Jacob rises from the stool and, assisted by Joseph, approaches Pharaoh, who signs to him to remain standing.

JOSEPH This is my father Israel, mighty Pharaoh! If
My father were to live ten thousand years
In great adversity, his faith would never fail.

KHYAN Jacob, welcome with your twelve fine sons!

JACOB More than sixty male descendants made
The journey into Egypt. We all thank
Your majesty for saving all our lives.

KHYAN Jacob, Israel, father of your son
The messenger of heaven, may I have
The blessing of so great a man?

JACOB Most certainly.
My blessing be on you, the Occupier
Of Egypt's Throne. As you have dealt with us,
In magnanimity, so may God give again to you!

KHYAN A noble blessing! Man of wisdom, what
Might be your age?

JACOB According to our
Computation this: A hundred and
Some thirty years – of a nomadic life
Of hardship and discomfort; *that* is my age.

KHYAN Every man in Egypt says: 'O to live
To be a hundred and ten!' – the age of our
Philosopher, great Ptahhotep. You have
Outstripped us. Will you intermarry with us?

JACOB (*courteously*) We'll remain apart. God will send to my
Posterity the inspiration that
Will lead them back to Canaan.

KHYAN Yes, ah yes, you are a race of seers.
Dreams will show you when to leave. Yes, I
Remember, in your youth, you saw Baal's ladder, which
Allows immortal souls to travel to the sun.

JACOB (*fiercely*) I saw the ladder of the only God, not Baal.

KHYAN (*calmly*) Religious strife is meaningless; *all*
Religions seek the Great Creator God.
Old, most venerable man – I am
Your host. You are my guest. My Egypt and
Your Hebron shall not quarrel over all
The different names of God.

JACOB (*sternly*) Our faith is in
The Shepherd God of Israel, who guides
His flock, who comforts and sustains his sheep.

KHYAN And our Osiris carries crook and harvest flail.
With deep respect I beg you: Bless me once again!

JACOB May God pour out his blessings on the Two
Lands ever after. Glorious Pharaoh, *this*
Is a momentous hour! You are king
Of mighty Egypt: We, we are founding fathers of
Our race, whose lives you've saved. Centuries
From now, we Hebrews shall be known as heroes of
The ancient time. Which all too human hero is
The greatest? Joseph, my dear son, without a doubt!

FINIS